Selling SUCKS

*How to Stop Selling
and Start Getting Prospects to Buy!*

FRANK J. RUMBAUSKAS JR.

John Wiley & Sons, Inc.

Published by John Wiley & Sons, Inc., Hoboken, New Jersey.
Published simultaneously in Canada.

Wiley Bicentennial Logo: Richard J. Pacifico.

For general information on our other products and services or for technical support, please contact our Customer Care Department within the United States at (800) 762-2974, outside the United States at (317) 572-3993, or fax (317) 572-4002.

Wiley also publishes its books in a variety of electronic formats. Some content that appears in print may not be available in electronic books. For more information about Wiley products, visit our web site at www.wiley.com.

Library of Congress Cataloging-in-Publication Data:

Rumbauskas, Frank J., 1973–
    Selling sucks : how to stop selling and start getting prospects to buy! / Frank J. Rumbauskas.
        p. cm.
    ISBN 978-0-470-11625-8 (cloth : alk. paper)
    1. Selling. I. Title.
    HF5438.25.R86 2007
    658.85—dc22

                                                                                2006102244

Printed in the United States of America.

10 9 8 7 6 5 4 3 2

To Dana,
the love of my life

CONTENTS

ACKNOWLEDGMENTS

Writing a book is a tremendous undertaking. I'm not talking about my effort. I spent enough time in sales, and now spend enough time teaching others and speaking about it, that putting my knowledge on paper isn't difficult. I could talk and write all day about sales—I love it!

The real work begins after I write the book and send it to the publisher, so I want to give credit where credit is due. Writing isn't all that difficult; transforming the raw manuscript into a finished book, and then getting it into stores and into the hands of readers, is what's hard.

First of all, my sincere thanks to the entire team at Wiley for their hard work. I'd particularly like to thank Matt Holt, who came up with the idea for this book and who encouraged me to write it; and Shannon Vargo, who discovered me in the first place and opened the line of communication that led to my first published book, *Never Cold Call Again: Achieve Sales Greatness Without Cold Calling.*

Speaking of *Never Cold Call Again*, I'd like to sincerely thank Dr. Joe Vitale for his help and genius in launching and promoting that book—without his help, it probably would not have made number one on Amazon, and certainly would not have appeared on the *New York Times* Best Seller List.

Credit must also go to Mark Joyner and Mike Filsaime for their advice and help with my Internet marketing efforts, another element without which I would have not achieved bestseller status; and, of course, to Tom Beal, who must be the greatest networker I've ever met and who introduced me to many of the powerful contacts I have today.

Love and thanks go to my family for their love and support over the years, especially when I decided to abandon the lifelong advice I'd received of "go to school, get a good job with a big company, and save money" and chose to do things my own way instead. Thank you for your support and understanding.

And finally, to Dana: Thank you for your love, understanding, and support. Thank you for being there.

PREFACE

I know what you're thinking. If selling sucks, you're in the wrong profession—you'll have to change careers!

Hold on—this isn't a book about careers. It's a book about selling; specifically, why selling is the worst possible way to get a sale.

It sounds crazy at first, doesn't it? It's not. After you read this book, you'll see very clearly why selling is the wrong answer if your goal is to make more sales. You may understand why that is in the first chapter, or it may take you longer to fully realize it, but either way, you're going to see very clearly that selling is a waste of time.

That's right. If you've been selling for a living, you've been wasting your time. You've been losing sales. You've even lost sales from people who wanted to buy from you at the start!

Did you catch what I just said there? They wanted to buy from you at the start . . . but instead of letting them buy, you started selling. . . .

Is it starting to make sense yet?

I will give you an example to help you understand what I'm getting at. Let's say you want salmon for dinner. There are two ways to get it. The first way is to book a trip to Alaska, spend thousands of dollars on the best fishing boat and equipment, go out and catch a salmon, clean it, and finally, cook it up for dinner.

The second way is to go to the nearest grocery story or fish market, and get yourself some salmon.

Both methods will get you the same result. Fortunately, you've been taught the second method, and therefore you will save yourself a lot of time and trouble.

The problem in the sales world, however, is that we're all taught to do things the first way. We're taught the hard way, the old-fashioned, "work for it" way, instead of the simple, practical method that will get us to our desired result with far less stress and hassle.

Are you ready to stop doing things the hard way, and start doing it the *right* way?

The old way just isn't worth it . . . the old way sucks. Selling sucks.

I never even knew there was a better way until about halfway through my sales career, and I stumbled upon the knowledge completely by accident. At the beginning, I was ordered to cold call. It didn't work, and over a period of a couple of years, I found ways to generate hot leads without cold calling. Suddenly, I had tons of qualified leads and my schedule was packed with appointments, but I didn't have nearly as many sales as I should have with all those prospects ready and willing to meet with me.

The problem was due to the fact that prospects who are

cold-called for an appointment expect to be sold at that appointment. You see, cold calling is a form of selling. When you start out by selling, they expect more selling. It's natural. They don't like it, but they expect it, and are not taken by surprise when you do it.

People who call you first, on the other hand, don't expect any selling. The big difference between cold call leads, and people who call *you* first, is that the people who call you first are highly qualified and very likely to buy. Not to be sold, to *buy*. When you start selling them, they are taken by surprise, caught off-guard, and, quite simply, are put off by it.

In fact, I don't think anyone likes to be dragged through the selling process. It's not fun and it's one big headache for everyone involved.

My sales went through the roof when I figured out how to stop selling and start getting people to buy. That's what Top Sales Pros do. They never sell—they simply create the circumstances for buying to take place, and then allow it to happen.

That reminds me—have you ever noticed that top sales pros keep to themselves, and never tell the rest of us just what it is they do to produce such tremendous sales numbers?

Can you blame them? Would you give your secrets away and create competition for yourself if you were a top sales pro?

Of course not . . . but in this book, you will learn the inside secrets of top sales pros. You'll learn what they do to be so successful. (Hint: It's not selling that they're doing.)

In the pages that follow, you're going to learn all of the things that top producers do to sell so much—and all of the things they don't do. You're going to get a glimpse inside the minds and activities of the very best of the best, and you'll learn how to take that knowledge and apply it for yourself, so that you, too, can become a top sales pro. You'll learn how to have power and control in all of your sales situations. You'll learn to establish yourself as a recognized expert in your industry, and get yourself written up in the news—literally overnight. You'll learn how to use the Internet as a lead-generator, in ways you've never even thought possible. You'll learn how to be featured at networking events as the main attraction, rather than just another attendee desperate for leads.

Becoming a top sales pro isn't hard. It's simply a matter of learning a skill set. There are no naturals. Top salespeople aren't the boss's best friend. They're simply following a skill set that anyone can learn, a simple series of tactics and techniques, that you will learn in this book.

Prepare to learn a new way of thinking as you go through the pages that follow. You're going to see the sales world through the eyes of a top sales pro, someone who sells more than double or triple what the average salesperson sells, yet with less effort. You're going to learn the skill set and the knowledge that top sales pros use and that is hidden from everyone else.

You're going to learn how to stop selling and start getting people to buy. And that's a good thing, because selling sucks.

1

IT'S TRUE—
SELLING SUCKS!

Yes, selling sucks. You know it and I know it. So why do we keep doing it?

Wait a minute—I mean why do *you* keep doing it? I don't sell anymore. In fact, I haven't in a very long time. That includes when I was still in sales, too. I became a top producer and stayed there consistently, without any selling. Then I got into sales training and sold obscene amounts of my sales training products and services, without selling. Finally, I became a best-selling author and sold tons of my books, without selling.

What about those sales superstars in your office, or in every office? They're usually accused of being the boss's friend and getting freebie leads tossed into their lap for nothing. I'm here to tell you that's simply not true. (And top sales pros hate it when people say that. So stop it!) Here's the truth: They're not living off of freebies, but they're not selling, either.

Stop! I know what you're thinking: "How on earth can anyone sell, without selling?"

It's easy. I'm looking around my office right now. When I bought the computer I am using to type this very book, the salesperson made a sale, but he didn't have to *sell* me. When I bought my car, I knew what I wanted and found out where to get it at a price I liked. The salesperson made a sale, but he didn't have to *sell* me. Every time Rush goes on tour and I go broke on front-row tickets, *I* call the ticket brokers and buy them. They sure don't have to *sell* me. In fact, I'm practically begging when I'm on the hunt for them.

And now you're probably thinking, "That's all well and good if you're talking about retail goods where people come strolling into a store. But, what about me? I'm in outside sales, Frank. I have to cold call. I have to set appointments. I spend half the day driving in my car to and from presentations. I *have* to sell. This won't work for me!"

Oh, how wrong you are.

As a business owner, I can tell you that this is even more applicable in business-to-business sales. I don't think we really disagree on this—I just think you and I have different interpretations of the word *sell*. You probably think *sell* means "to make a sale." In my world, it's the word *buy* that actually means "to make a sale."

And in my world, *selling* suggests an uphill battle of trying to convince someone to buy from you when they really don't want to, are not a well-qualified prospect, have no clearly defined need for your product or service, or simply do not care to meet with you. And, unfortunately, this describes the vast majority of sales appointments.

In my world, when I think of the word *selling*, I picture cold calling, blitzes, elevator speeches, initial benefit statements, pushing prospects for appointments, overcoming objections, and sleazy closes like the alternate close or the Ben Franklin close. This is how nearly all salespeople are taught to sell.

Ick. I think I need a shower now. Just the thought of it all makes me feel dirty.

Now, picture this. Imagine having a nonstop supply of hot, qualified leads coming to you every day. Imagine calling those leads back and hearing their excitement at the opportunity to meet with you. Think of how easy it is when you sail through the meeting with no interruptions, get the prospect's agreement on everything you say, and walk out with a signed order and a check—oh, and with no price objections. You just made a sale—but you weren't *selling*.

You see, selling is only necessary when you're in front of someone who doesn't necessarily want to buy from you. But when they *do* want to buy from you, everything happens so smoothly.

When they want to buy from you, you don't work against them. You work with them. When they want to buy from you, you don't have to overcome objections. You simply fill a need. When they want to buy from you, price is not an issue. When they want to buy from you, they just buy—you don't have to sell them!

Do you now understand what I mean when I say top producers don't sell? Sales superstars don't have to, because they are masters of attracting prospects who are ready and willing to buy, and they simply allow the sale to take place. A top sales pro is like the conductor leading the orchestra, rather than one of the players physically engaged in playing the music. Top sales pros put the pieces into place, then gently lead everything in the direction they want it all to go. And that means attracting prospects who are ready to buy, then inducing them to go ahead and do it. No cold calls. No initial benefit statements. No being pushy. No pissing anyone off. No making enemies. No ethically questionable closing tactics.

Just a sale.

I've been accused by my critics of turning salespeople into order takers. To them I say, what sane salesperson does *not* want to become an order taker? What I'm really doing is getting salespeople to stop selling, and turning them into top sales pros who know how to create the conditions for a sale to take place without selling—just buying.

If you'd rather live a stress-filled life selling, fighting an up-hill battle of trying to push and convince people to buy from you, then go right ahead. You don't need this book. But if you want to learn how to become a top sales pro who never has to sell because you create the proper conditions for people to come to you and simply buy, keep reading.

I've dissected every facet of what a top sales pro does, day in and day out—every last detail. I've reverse engineered what I and other sales superstars did and continue to do every day to stay on top, and we do it without getting high blood pressure or stomach ulcers or working 12-hour days. In fact, you'll find that being a top sales pro is actually *easy*, once you know how.

There's an unfortunate myth that great salespeople are born, not made. That's simply not true. Top salespeople are made, through knowledge, and by learning to acquire the skill set of a top salesperson.

The fact that this is all simply a skill set that anyone can learn and implement is wonderful news. I read a book recently by Neil Strauss, entitled *The Game: Penetrating the Secret Society of Pickup Artists* (New York: Regan Books, 2005). It's a true story of how Neil, your quintessential nerd who could not get a woman to talk to him to save his life, set out on a quest to become a great "pickup artist." He spent over two years studying, learning, going to seminars, attending workshops, and going out night after night practicing his newfound skills. In a surprisingly short time, he became known as the world's greatest pickup artist. He eventually dropped out of "the game" when he met and fell in love with a beautiful celebrity girlfriend, the kind most men only dream about.

Now, most people will tell you that a great pickup artist is born, not made. Most everyone will tell you that no one can go from being a short, awkward nerd to a ladies' man who is literally revered by other men, very quickly, simply by studying and learning a skill set. But he did it. And you can, too. (In sales, of course! The pickup arts were just an example!)

I was a shy introvert when I started out in sales, and believe me, it was extremely difficult. However, by simply learning a skill set, I became an unstoppable sales machine, a top sales pro. I didn't have to change my personality or who I was at the core. I just needed some practical knowledge—the skill set of the masters.

You won't have to change, either. You just have to learn a new skill set. You will find the skill set of top sales pros in this book, presented in such a way that you will be able to quickly assimilate and begin using the information immediately.

Your days of the drudgery of selling are over. Welcome to the secret society of top sales pros. Hey, I'm not being all that dramatic—you know as well as I do that they won't tell you their secrets to sales stardom! After all, why would they want competition? But I *will* tell you their secrets, so let's begin.

2

TOP SALES PROS ARE MASTER PERSUADERS

Are you a master persuader? Notice I didn't say master *salesperson*. I said master *persuader*.

You see, a top sales pro doesn't sell. Selling is an uphill battle of trying to convince someone to buy when they don't want to or perhaps don't need to. In other words, even though you've made sales in the past by selling, the fact is that many of the people you've sold to may not have really wanted to buy from you. You just happened to do a great job of selling them, or pressuring them until they gave in. Selling is only necessary when the prospect does not *want* to buy.

A great persuader, on the other hand, makes people *want to buy*! That's the difference between a seller and a persuader. The seller never actually makes the prospect want to buy—he simply coerces him into buying through a series of steps intended to do just that. These steps usually include a lot of the old-school sales lingo we've all had forced down our throats, such as *initial benefit statements, elevator speeches, cold calls*, a whole multitude of potentially unethical *closes*, and on and on. By now I'm sure you've heard it all.

Dave Lakhani made the distinction very clear in his excellent book, *Persuasion: The Art of Getting What You Want* (Hoboken, NJ: John Wiley & Sons, 2005). Dave actually describes the differences between persuasion and manipulation—for all intents and purposes, manipulation and selling are the same.

Here's the key difference, as Dave explains it: Manipulation is getting someone to do something for your benefit. Persuasion is getting someone to do something for your *mutual* benefit.

Think about that for a minute, and think about why you've made the sales you've made. Did you make sales because you were helping people? Or did you make sales because they resulted in a commission check?

Be totally honest here. Think about what your *primary* motivation is when making sales. Sure, you may have honestly helped customers here and there, but wasn't your primary motivation actually just the commission, and not the satisfaction of having fulfilled a business need—having solved the prospect's problem, thereby turning that prospect into a customer?

As I write this I'm sitting on a plane, traveling home from New York. I spent the past week brainstorming and masterminding with Internet marketing legends Mike Filsaime and Tom Beal. One of the greatest revelations for me over the past week is that Mike has become a multimillionaire extremely quickly by giving his knowledge away, for free!

This was completely amazing to me at first because of the obvious fact that Mike is in the information business. In other words, his income is derived from the sale of information products that teach others how to become successful Internet marketers. Common sense says that Mike would make the most money by hoarding his knowledge and only granting access to it to those who pay for it, but in reality, Mike has become far more successful by giving it away and trusting that people would come back and eventually buy his other products and services!

How can this be?

Well, to put it quite simply, the law of compensation is always at work around us. This law simply states that checks and balances exist everywhere, and that the best way to receive great riches is to first give, with no expectation of reward.

Again, how can this be?

In the case of information marketers such as Mike—and myself, for that matter—when we give away a free e-book or CD or video, people see the quality of our products and are eager to come back for more. That's why they are so willing to come back and buy products that are frequently very expensive. The thought process is, "Wow, if his free products are this good, his for-sale products must be really great!"

If Mike and I were to hoard our knowledge, on the other

hand, it would be far more difficult to convince people to buy anything at all. Buying an information product without at least seeing a preview is like buying a car without test-driving it. Would you do that? Unless you're buying a Bentley or Ferrari, which you already know is good, the chances are slim. (The concept of not having to test-drive the Bentley before buying it is covered in Chapter 9. Once you become the recognized expert in your prospects' eyes, they will buy from you without the test-drive, just like you would a Bentley. They will assume you are the best without the need for references or, in this example, a test-drive.)

Manipulation is bad. It's done only to serve your own interests, without any regard to whether what you are doing is good for the prospect. Don't get me wrong here—I'm all for making money, and that's the main reason I'm in business myself. But I'm totally, 100 percent against making money at the expense of another person. Profit is only good when the product sold benefits the purchaser. In the case of information products, the purchaser cannot determine whether the product will be useful unless they get a preview; hence the free e-books.

Persuasion, however, is good, not only because it is done for the best interests of both the seller *and* the prospect, but also because persuasion is built on a foundation of honesty and integrity.

You'll notice that I come back to those two words, *honesty* and *integrity*, throughout this book. They are the starting point, the foundation upon which you must build if you ever want to become a top sales pro. Instead of trying to define them the dictionary way, I'll give some examples of honesty and integrity in selling.

The first is *setting realistic expectations*—not making promises you can't keep. When I was new to sales, I constantly made promises I couldn't keep. For example, when I sold business telephone systems, I constantly promised that I'd be able to meet installation deadlines that I knew very well I could not. I only made the promise because I thought I'd lose the sale if I didn't. It is very common for a business that is moving to wait until the very last minute to order the phone system. As a result, they needed installation fast—very fast. When they asked if I could do it in the two days or so that they needed, I said, "Yes, sir!" I thought I had to in order to get the contract signed. I was a yes-man. I made every promise I could come up with just to get the sale.

Later on, when I became more successful, more confident, and wasn't desperate for each and every sale anymore, I decided to try something different—honesty. What a novel concept! Instead of saying, "Yes, sir!" I said, "Unfortunately, I cannot meet that date. I can have it done in a week, but not two days. I'll understand if you must go with a different vendor as a result."

What happened next astounded me: I got more sales when I said no! When I told them that I could not meet their expectations, and that I would understand if they did not buy from me, they bought. The reason for this is also quite sad. Prospects are used to liars and are so amazed at hearing honesty from a salesperson that they will jump at the opportunity to do business with that person. There is such a lack of honesty and integrity out there that prospects will never expect this level of honesty from you, and, as a result, they will want to do business with you and no one else. Honesty is persuasion at its finest.

I derived another tremendous benefit from my newfound honesty, which brings me to my next point: *Break bad news to customers immediately.* The worst thing about making promises that I couldn't keep was having to break the news to my new customers. After saying yes, I was forced to pick up the phone and say, "I'm sorry, but they were not able to get the installation date I promised." Notice how I used the word *they*—I certainly wasn't about to take the blame, even though it was all the result of my lie! I passed the buck to the company, the management, the union, you name it. Everyone but me was at fault. The customers, however, knew better. They're so used to dishonesty from salespeople that they knew right away that I'd lied at the start. It wasn't the company's fault. As you can imagine, I didn't get any referrals from those customers.

When I became honest and set realistic expectations, I had to break bad news to customers far, far less often than I had to in the past. And, because they loved and appreciated my honesty, they didn't beat me up when I did have bad news. They understood. They accepted the fact that these things happen. And the best part is that they appreciated me even more for immediately telling them the bad news and accepting responsibility for it, instead of trying to cover it up or avoid blame or pass it on to someone else. It was very easy to get hot referrals from these people.

It's important to remember that people who report a very

high level of customer satisfaction aren't the ones who have had no problems at all. They're usually the ones who did experience problems, but who were informed of those problems immediately and had them resolved to a positive outcome. What I'm saying here is that breaking bad news to a customer is actually an opportunity to make them love you even more!

A third example of honesty and integrity is *admitting that your solution may not be the best fit.* I remember when a company I'd worked for did a big direct mail campaign. Our fliers told prospects to call us to schedule a free consultation with a representative. It was a total crock of you-know-what, because the so-called recommendation at the end of the consultation was to buy our products.

A real consultant isn't biased like that. Real consultants make honest, unbiased recommendations based upon what solutions will best serve their clients.

Imagine what goes through a prospect's mind when a salesperson who has already spent significant time with them going through a sales process recommends someone else's solution. Chances are, it's the first time they've ever experienced that, and it will likely be the last. Most salespeople are out to make a sale for their own benefit. They don't want to put the prospect's best interests first and risk losing a potential sale.

When you are totally and completely honest and actually recommend a competitor's solution, two things happen. First, the prospect is absolutely floored by your honesty. Like I said, this has never happened before. In almost every case, you will get the sale anyway, because all they've ever wanted was a salesperson with that level of honesty and integrity! Second, they're going to rave about you to everyone they know. You'll never have to ask for referrals, because they will become your ready and willing referral partners. Sort of kills two birds with one stone, doesn't it?

Now that you've seen some good examples of what I mean by honesty and integrity, let's get back to how this relates to being a master persuader. Since persuasion is done with the prospect's best interests in mind, it only makes sense that it must begin on a foundation of honesty and integrity. As Dave Lakhani points out, intent is the only thing that separates manipulation from persuasion. The manipulator is focused only on his own benefit. The persuader is focused on creating a win-win situation that benefits everyone involved.

When you constantly have a mind-set of working from a foundation of honesty and integrity, and focusing on benefiting the prospect in order to create a win-win situation, something interesting happens. You begin to internalize these principles, and you unknowingly convey them to prospects. You do that through subcommunication.

Subcommunication simply refers to the unspoken communication we're all transmitting to others, without even realizing it. A 1972 U.C.L.A. study concluded that 93 percent of our communication is nonverbal. That means that the words we say account for only 7 percent of our communication and the other 93 percent comes from our posture and position, vocal inflection and tone, movement of the body, and other nonverbal cues. This is common knowledge to both psychologists and persuasion experts.

Your nonverbal subcommunication largely comes from

your mind-set and the ideals on which you operate. If you operate from a position of dishonesty, or self-interest without regard to the prospect's interests, you automatically display insecurity because you know very well that you're not really the person you represent yourself to be. Your nonverbal communication conveys this, and prospects pick up on it. They don't trust you and don't want to do business with you. They don't know why—to them it's just a gut feeling that they can't quite pinpoint—but the bottom line is that they've judged you as untrustworthy, and you're through.

By contrast, when you operate from a position of integrity, honesty, and seeking to create a win-win outcome that benefits the prospect as well as yourself, your nonverbal communication conveys an air of confidence, power, respect, prestige, and trust. The higher your ethics, and the longer you have been practicing those ethics, the stronger your nonverbal communication becomes. Prospects will want to be around you and will want to do business with you. As in the previous example, they won't know exactly why—they may simply describe you as "likeable"—but who cares if they know why or not? The bottom line is that you're going to get the sale, and future sales, and referrals!

Going back to the beginning of this chapter, it's quite easy to see how a master persuader makes people want to buy! When you're working from a foundation of integrity, with their interests in mind, of course they will want to buy from you! However, if you're trying to sell them—manipulate them—they will know it, they will feel like they're being sold, and they *will not* want to buy.

Master persuaders are top sales pros because people want to buy from master persuaders whom they know they can trust. Follow the principles in this chapter to become a master persuader and watch your sales explode! At www.NeverColdCall.com/Secrets you'll find more examples of how you can persuade others instead of manipulating them.

3

TOP SALES PROS DON'T COLD CALL

That's right, top sales pros don't cold call!

Wait a minute! Haven't we all been taught that cold calling is the key to success, and that not cold calling is a guaranteed way to fail at a career in sales? Isn't the mantra to increase your activity and make 50 calls a day the shortcut to riches?

Wrong!

I've covered this topic extensively in my previous book, *Never Cold Call Again: Achieve Sales Greatness Without Cold Calling*, so I won't go too deeply into it here. However, it's important to understand why cold calling is actually the path to failure, and why top sales pros absolutely, without exception, do not cold call. So let's touch on the main reasons why it's a very bad idea.

First of all, cold calling simply does not work anymore in today's economy. Sure, it will get you an appointment and even a sale here and there, but have you considered the horrible inefficiency of cold calling? Let's face it—on average, less than one percent of cold calls actually result in a qualified lead. The key word here is *qualified*—cold calling will get you appointments, all right, but they tend to be the worst quality prospects you can possibly get! They're the ones who get you all excited by saying, "This looks great, we think we're going to do it," then mysteriously disappear and never return another phone call.

What are the long-term consequences of spending your valuable time on an activity that has such an extremely low rate of return? It's really quite simple. Time is money, but unlike money, time can never be replaced. Once it's spent, it's gone forever. Therefore, spending your time on the activity with the absolute lowest rate of return is a guaranteed way to fail. That's why top sales pros don't do it.

Top sales pros are able to get to the top and stay there by maximizing their time. This doesn't necessarily mean so-called time management but, rather, spending time solely on the activities that yield the highest rate of return, much like a great investor only considers investments that give the highest returns. Every time you make a decision as to how you will spend your time, you are investing in your future—and let's face it, your time and your future are far more valuable than the dollars a professional investor spends his time investing. So, with that in mind, you should invest your time with at least as much caution as a professional investor uses in investing his money. Investing your time in low-percentage activities like cold calling will never make you a top sales pro.

I get tons of e-mails from people who insist that cold calling works. Sure, it works. Just like a bicycle and a Rolls-Royce will both get you from point A to point B, but somehow people still shell out a quarter-million or more for the Rolls instead of choosing the $50 bicycle.

Here's an analogy for how well cold calling works. I'm a car detail nut. I like my car to always look outstanding, with a brilliant, deep shine. I could achieve this shine the old-fashioned, "wax on, wax off" way. It would take hours and hours of massive effort and would leave me exhausted and sore afterward. However, it would get the desired result.

Another way to make my car look amazing is to pick up the machine polisher and use that instead. In one-fourth of the time it takes to detail the car by hand, I can achieve an even better finish, with far less effort!

That's the difference between cold calling and self-marketing. Cold calling may work, but it's like detailing the car by hand. Why would I bother when it's so much easier and far more efficient to use the machine?

The second reason top sales pros absolutely do not cold call is less obvious, yet far more insidious. Rather than try to explain it, I'll have you look through the eyes of a prospect, because learning to think like your prospects is the fastest way to understand what makes them buy and how you can quickly get them buying from *you*.

In Chapter 2, I mentioned that even though you would absolutely want to test-drive a car before buying it, if you had the money you would likely buy a new car such as a Ferrari or Bentley without the need for a test-drive. After all, these automobile brands are legendary, and it's pretty much a given that you'd be happy with your purchase were you to buy one of these cars.

Now, what if you were looking at a beat-up, used Ford Escort? Imagine for a moment that it is the only car you can afford, you don't have enough money to correct a mistake, and you absolutely must make the right decision the first time around. Would you test-drive that beat-up Ford Escort? Of course you would! In fact, even if the seller made you an amazing deal on the price of the car, I'm willing to bet that you still would not buy it without a test-drive.

Keeping this analogy in mind, think of a prospect's perception of two different salespeople. The first salesperson has already established a tremendous amount of credibility before going into the sales situation and is recognized as an expert by the prospect. By contrast, the second salesperson is not seen by the prospect as a recognized expert and has not done anything to establish credibility with the prospect. In fact, the prospect's only contact with this salesperson has been through a cold call. Which salesperson will be viewed as the Bentley and which will be viewed as a beat-up Ford Escort?

The answer is obvious. The first salesperson—the recognized expert who has established credibility in advance—is the Bentley. But the cold caller is automatically assumed to have the same level of quality and reliability as a beat-up Ford Escort.

Taking this a step further, the prospect will buy from the first salesperson, the Bentley, without a test-drive. A test-drive is not necessary because quality and reputation are assumed in advance. However, there is no way any intelligent prospect will buy from a cold caller, the beat-up Ford Escort, without a very thorough test-drive and complete inspection.

Why is this so? Quite simply, it's because the mere need to cold call creates an image of desperation and failure. A top sales pro absolutely cannot cold call because doing so will totally obliterate any credibility and trust the pro has brought to the table in advance. Later in this book you will learn how to become *the* recognized expert in your field. Prospects will seek you out and will be eager to buy from you (no selling required) just because of the image and credibility you will have created in advance. Now, consider what would happen to that immense credibility were you to cold call those very same prospects.

Again, look at this through the prospect's eyes. Imagine that a very well-known, reputable attorney lives in your community. What would happen if that same attorney knocked on your door tomorrow morning, complete with an elevator speech explaining who he is and what he does, an initial benefit statement telling you why it is in your best interests to meet with him, and, finally, a push to get an appointment with you? What would happen to that attorney's credibility in your mind? Would you still see him as the same powerful, respected attorney you did before his cold call?

Of course not. Even though he'd spent decades building a track record and a reputation of being the very best, all of that would be discredited just because he cold called you. It's common knowledge that the best of the best have no need to cold call. This is equally true for the top attorney and for top sales pros.

A third reason why top sales pros don't cold call is closely related to the second reason. In order to have the respect and trust of valuable, highly qualified prospects, you must be seen as a business equal or, even better, a business superior. You want prospects to see you as someone to whom they can turn for advice. By entering every sales situation from such a position, you control the entire sales process right from the start and are able to guide that sales process to the conclusion you want—a sale.

Here's the bottom line: *Cold calling destroys your status as a business equal.* When your initial contact with a prospect is via a cold call, you position yourself as a business inferior right from the start. You are seen as a supplicant by the prospect, and, as a result, you are most definitely not someone to whom they want to entrust their important matters.

There's a very good reason that many top sales pros display the fact that they are on top. We've all seen "President's Club" or something similar on business cards. Are they doing it to brag? No! It's because top sales pros know that people want to do business with people who are successful. An established record of success conveys a lot of positive things about you; most importantly, it conveys that you provide value to your customers, and that you have honesty and integrity. Sales success presumes these things, and prospects know it. Therefore, they strongly prefer to buy from someone who is already successful, not from someone who is desperate to make a sale in order to survive.

When you make a cold call, do you look successful or desperate? The answer is obvious, and it influences the mind of the prospect more than you can imagine. Even when you manage to find qualified leads by cold calling, you're automatically at a strong disadvantage to the pros who are competing for the sale, who did not make the initial contact with a cold call.

A fourth big reason why cold calling is ineffective is that it is a huge time waster. Trying to approach people at random with the hope that they might have a need for your product or service is horribly inefficient. It's the worst possible way to attempt to generate leads, when you have no idea whether the people you are approaching have a need to begin with, or are even qualified to buy.

The old admonition to "increase your activity" only makes the situation worse, because it encourages you to do more of something that doesn't work in the first place. The answer isn't to increase your activity—it's to *change* your activity to something that does work! I learned at a young age that any number times zero equals zero. So if an activity gets you a zero result, how on earth does it makes sense to do even more of it? Fifty times zero still equals zero! That's why this admonition is sheer insanity.

If you want to be a top sales pro, you need to stop cold calling and start using intelligent systems of self-marketing to generate leads. Cold calling demolishes your credibility and trustworthiness and wastes your time. Don't do it.

4

Top Sales Pros Get and Keep the Power

If I had to choose one thing that separates top sales pros from total sales failures, it's power. Top sales pros have tremendous power, and failures absolutely do not, so this chapter is very important—perhaps the most important in the book.

As I progressed through my sales career, I went from cold calling with no results to creating systems of self-marketing that generated leads on autopilot for me, without any need to proactively prospect on my part. I ran into a problem, though. When I went out to meet with those leads, they were put off by the way I carried myself. Even though I had successfully stopped cold calling, I continued to carry out the rest of the sales process in the old-fashioned way I'd been taught, over and over again.

The problem lies with the fact that the old-school methods of selling tend to put salespeople in a position of weakness and put prospects in a position of power. This is absolutely disastrous to sales results. Top sales pros have the power all along—they get it right at the start of the sales process, and keep it all the way through to the end and beyond. The problem is that salespeople are typically taught to give away all their power. Before I explain why, though, it's important to understand the concept of power in selling.

What is power? First you must understand that every contact you make with a prospective customer is a negotiation. Whether you're making an initial contact, setting an appointment, conducting an appointment, presenting, or what have you, every sales interaction is a negotiation. This is true whether it's done in person, on the phone, via e-mail, or through any other medium. Even your marketing pieces are a negotiation. They're trying to convince prospects to call you, and the prospects are trying to decide whether it's in their best interest to do so.

Quite simply, the person who has the power in a negotiation will lead that negotiation to his desired end.

Who holds the power is determined by who has the greater need. In every sales interaction—and in every negotiation, for that matter—the person who has a need does not have the power and therefore is not in control. The person who can fulfill a need, however, has all of the power and will control the entire interaction all the way to the very end.

Think of what it's like to go into a bank and apply for a loan. The bank clearly has the power and will decide how the interaction will end. This is simply because you have the need—you need a loan—and the bank has the power to either fulfill or deny that need. You gave them that power by stating your desire to get the loan.

How does this concept apply to selling? Remember, the person with the need does not have the power—the power lies with the person who can fulfill a need. When you approach a prospect in a cold call situation, it is very clear to the prospect that you are in need of a sale; you have a need. (Whether you think you are in need is irrelevant; what matters here is the prospect's perception of you, and they perceive you as being in need.) By communicating this need to the prospect, you have automatically and unknowingly placed the prospect into the very powerful position of either fulfilling or denying that need.

Knowing that the prime determinant of power lies in coming from a position of being able to fulfill a need, rather than having a need yourself, the key at the beginning is *positioning*. You must position yourself as being a provider who can fulfill a need rather than as a salesperson who needs a sale. You do this by marketing yourself and your products and services in such a way that prospects call you, rather than you cold calling prospects. That's how you get the power at the start.

Once you establish yourself in a position of power at the beginning of the sales process, it's equally important to maintain that position of power throughout the entire process, all the way to the end. As I mentioned earlier, I wasn't closing sales at a sufficient rate once I had perfected my prospecting systems and had leads pouring in. I was failing because I was supplicating my prospects. Why? Because that's what I had been told to do all along. Like most salespeople, I perceived prospects as my superiors, and I treated them as such. The end result was that I lost all of my power—no matter how powerful I had appeared at the beginning of the interaction—which resulted in the prospect taking control, and me losing the sale.

Remember, you have one singular goal as the outcome of

every sales interaction, and that's to get a sale at the highest possible profit margin. You need to stay in power to attain that goal. If you lose your power, your prospect will then have control and will steer the interaction toward one of two goals that all prospects have: either to get rid of you, if they don't want to buy, or to buy from you at a price that is so unacceptably low as to destroy your profit margin.

How can you keep your power throughout the entire sales interaction? You do it by avoiding supplicant behaviors and by acting like a true professional—like a CEO or business owner would act. Those people, if they are successful, don't supplicate others. In a moment we'll look at some specific points in this regard, but first let's review what subcommunication is.

As explained in Chapter 2, when we think of how we communicate with others, we tend to focus on our outward communication—the words we say. In fact, most of what you'll learn in traditional sales training and books consists of only words. However, the words we use are only a very small part of our overall communication. The well-publicized U.C.L.A. study that I mentioned earlier concluded that the words we say account for only 7 percent of our overall communication! The other 93 percent consists of body language and voice quality. It's that nonverbal 93 percent that I refer to as subcommunication. With that in mind, here are some specifics tips for using your communication and your subcommunication to maintain your power in sales interactions.

AVOID PHONY RAPPORT

For some reason, salespeople are consistently taught to build phony rapport with prospects, usually by picking out some random thing in the prospect's office, like an award or photo, and then attempting to use that to build a conversation. Prospects see right through this because they know you are both there for business.

Be friendly and affable, but get down to business—don't waste the prospect's time with phony rapport. Getting right to the point in a friendly, approachable manner is a lot more professional and is appreciated by professionals.

AVOID PHONY OR CANNED LANGUAGE

Plowing through a canned presentation, complete with canned phrases such as, "More profit is something you'd like to achieve, don't you agree, Mr. Prospect?" only makes you look like someone who is too afraid and too insecure to be a real person who conducts real conversations.

In my live presentations, I ask everyone in the audience to get up out of their chairs and get as close to the stage as possible. I then explain that by seeing me up close and personal, they realize that I'm a real human being, not some distant character playing a part. It's easy for someone sitting in the audience to watch me on stage and feel disconnected, as if they were watching an actor on television. Getting up close, however, builds a personal connection that remains throughout the rest of the presentation. That's why I do it at the beginning.

The same is true for you in sales appointments. Show your prospects that you're a real person, not an automaton going through the motions, forgetting that both you and the prospect are human. Nothing will make you appear more inhuman than silly, canned lines like, "Don't you agree?" and "Does that sound fair?"

There's another very big reason to avoid this kind of language. It has to do with the fact that most business owners and executives of today were the salespeople of yesterday. Guess what? The phony lines I just mentioned come from the sales books of yesterday, which, of course, means that most of your prospects have read those books and have used those lines themselves. The number one reason why old-school sales tactics don't work anymore is because the prospects of today have used and know those tactics! They can spot them a mile away! It's insulting to a person to know that lines are being used on them in place of sincere conversation, so don't do it. It's a sure way to lose sales fast.

SLOW DOWN

The mark of the powerless, nervous individual is talking too fast. Talking too fast subcommunicates that you are worried that your prospect will lose interest and stop listening. In other words, weak salespeople are afraid that the prospect will cut them off and end the interaction soon, so they say everything they intend to say as quickly as possible, before that can happen!

If you observe powerful, confident people, you'll notice that they do not talk fast. They are relaxed in their speech and do not rush their words, and that conveys confidence and trust. The same is true for their mannerisms—they move more slowly than less-confident people and are never in a hurry. It's just as important to avoid quick, fidgety movements—and not seem to be in a hurry—as it is to avoid talking too quickly. By slowing down both your speech and your movements, you increase the level of confidence and power you subcommunicate, and that in turn causes prospects to see you as a powerful individual whom they can trust.

DON'T SAY "RIGHT?" OR "YOU KNOW?" AFTER STATEMENTS

One of the hallmarks of powerful people is that they never need to seek the validation of others. They know they're powerful and confident and they don't need anyone to reassure them of that.

When you say "Right?" or "You know?" at the end of your sentences, what you're really doing, in the prospect's eyes, is seeking their validation. You're asking them to approve what you've just said. It's like asking, "Am I acceptable to you? Please, please validate me!" after each sentence! Now how is *that* going to give you any power?

When you end your sentences, do so powerfully and with full confidence that what you've just said is exactly what the prospect wanted to hear.

TAKE AS MUCH SPACE AS YOU NEED

Powerful people take up space. Watch Donald Trump the next time you see him on television. He leans back, spreads out, and stakes his claim on wherever he happens to be sitting or standing. Weak, needy people are afraid to take up space. They keep their feet close together and their arms close to their body. They rarely lean back and spread out.

When you take up too little space, you subcommunicate that you are afraid of infringing on the prospect's space. Prospects interpret this as fear, and you thereby give them all of your power. Relax, spread out, and be powerful!

KEEP YOUR HANDS CALM WHILE TALKING

This is a tough one to explain to salespeople, because most have been wrongfully taught that moving your hands around a lot while you talk is a form of expressiveness. I'll tell you what it really means in the world of body language subcommunication: Moving your hands around while talking indicates a release of nervous energy and tension.

Are powerful people nervous? Of course not! Confident people are relaxed and do not need to release nervous energy. Think of the hero characters in a novel or a movie. They're always portrayed as standing with their hands on their hips or resting at their sides. Can you imagine a powerful hero character moving their hands all about while talking?

Don't buy into the myth that moving your hands around in gestures while talking is expressive. It's really a sign of weakness, and it won't help you get any sales.

LEANING IN EQUALS WEAKNESS

I've already mentioned leaning back in my Donald Trump example. Powerful people lean back. Needy people lean in toward whomever they're speaking with.

Every time I bring this up in a live presentation, someone always asks, "Aren't we supposed to mirror prospects, and lean in when they lean back?" No. Mirroring is another story altogether—it's something I don't recommend but I won't get into it here. However, any time you lean in, you are supplicating, especially if it's in a mirroring situation where you are following the prospect. Powerful people don't follow—they lead.

Leaning back is a basic part of powerful body language, so

begin doing it. And if you're leaning in because people can't hear you, speak up! That brings me to my next point.

HAVE A POWERFUL, COMMANDING VOICE

Voice quality takes up nearly half of that 93 percent of our nonverbal communication. Your voice tone matters. That means the volume of your voice (vocal projection), the tone of your voice, and its inflection. Weak people speak quietly, for the same reason they take up little space—they're afraid of infringing on others. Powerful people speak powerfully and confidently and are heard clearly.

It's easy to go overboard here. Talking very loudly to the point where you seem to be saying, "Look at me!" is almost as bad as speaking too softly. However, practice having a clear, powerful voice that carries and that will make you heard. Having to repeat yourself isn't powerful and it interrupts the flow of your appointments.

The hands-down best way to create a powerful voice is through public speaking. If this isn't a skill you possess yet—and it's a skill that all top sales pros possess—take a public speaking class or join Toastmasters. Not only will your voice improve, but so will your confidence and your ability to present. These are skills that help immensely not only in sales but in all areas of life.

WITHDRAW FROM A PROSPECT'S DISRESPECTFUL BEHAVIOR

Let's face it. There are jerks out there in the world, and some of them wind up being our prospects. I sure had my share of them. They have a self-important attitude, and nothing seems to bring out their shallow self-importance like a meeting with a sales rep. I've spent enough time in sales to have plenty of prospects try and walk all over me. Even now, it still happens sometimes when I'm dealing with an especially insecure person who has an overwhelming need to feel important. Don't ever put up with this sort of behavior.

Prospects like this continue to get away with their behavior because 99 percent of salespeople put up with it. They're so desperate for the sale—are *in need* of the sale—that they will take all kinds of abuse so long as they still have a chance of winning the sale. I'm telling you right now that top sales pros *never* take abuse from prospects, ever.

Two things happened when I started to put my foot down with disrespectful prospects. First, my confidence shot through the roof. When I stood up for myself against rude prospects, I internalized that behavior, and it became a part of me. Second, I got more sales! Keep in mind that people who act self-important are very weak deep down inside. Their self-important behavior is all a façade, intended to prevent you from seeing their weakness and to trick you into thinking they're strong. By calling them out on this behavior, they shrink down into the weaklings they are, obey you, and hand you all of their power.

I've had more than one instance where I was in the middle of a presentation and the prospect answered the phone, began typing on a computer, or did something else to interrupt me. When I suddenly closed my binder, stood up, and announced, "I think we need to reschedule this meeting for a time when I'll have your full attention," they stuttered and stammered and said, "No, now is fine, I'll pay attention from now on," and they did. I usually got the sale after that, along with their full respect. Remember, fake boldness equals internal weakness. Call them out on it and you gain control of the situation. Never accept behavior from a prospect that you would not accept from anyone else.

ANSWER QUESTIONS IN YOUR OWN TIME FRAME

When prospects interrupt your presentation with questions, and you stop right in the middle to answer them, you show that you are too eager to get the sale. You appear needy.

The powerful thing to do is to say, "I appreciate your question. What I'd like to do is go through my presentation, and then address your questions and concerns at the end, when we can revisit any areas you're unsure about."

FINISH YOUR PRESENTATION BEFORE
REVISITING UNFINISHED POINTS

This is related to the previous point. If you get cut off during your appointment—for instance, by a question, or if the prospect must interrupt you to take an important phone call—and then you immediately go back to what you were saying before, you again appear too eager for the sale and too eager to impress the prospect.

After an interruption, resume the appointment by moving on to the next point that was on your list, and be willing to go back and revisit the point you were making or the question you were asking later on, after you are finished.

STATE THINGS BRIEFLY AND SIMPLY

Don't take too long to state something that can be said in fewer words. Let's say, for example, that a prospect asks me, "Frank, can your product take care of all four points we discussed?"

I can answer with, "Yes, Mr. Prospect, we can handle point one, point two, point three, and point four, with the best service of anyone in our industry, just like we did for ABC Company down the street and so many other customers." Or I can answer with, "Yes, we can do that." Which one sounds confident, and which one sounds like I was trying too hard?

When you use too many words to say something that can be stated simply, you appear to be trying too hard to impress the prospect. That's weak. The less you say, the more confident and profound you appear to be.

BE CONFIDENT RATHER THAN BOLD

Take a skydiving example: Skydiver number one is getting ready to jump, and yells, "Woohoo! Yeaaahhhhhh! This is going to be *awesome! Yeaaahhhhh!*" That's boldness.

Skydiver number two says, "Okay, here we go—I'll see you guys on the ground." That's confidence.

Be confident, not bold. Boldness implies that you are overcompensating for insecurities. Confidence conveys confidence, plain and simple.

DON'T OVERCOMPENSATE FOR INSECURITIES

Here's an example of how I used to overcompensate for my insecurities before I learned all of this: Every now and then, against my own advice, I'd get lazy in the morning and dress in casual clothes instead of putting on a nice suit. When I went to appointments that day, I'd say something to the effect of, "I'm sorry I'm dressed down. I had to go out to a construction site today and didn't want to get one of my suits all dirty."

That's weak. The powerful thing to do is to not bring it up at all. When you bring attention to a shortcoming and try to explain it away, all you're doing is showing that you're feeling insecure about it. Just don't bring it up. Whether your clothes are casual or your car is dirty or you didn't shave that day, just don't bring it up. Act like everything is perfectly fine, and it will be.

DON'T OVERCOMPENSATE FOR FAILURES

Again, here's an example of something I used to do that was dead wrong: If I was conducting an appointment that wasn't going well, I'd yawn and say, "Wow, I'm really tired today." Doing so subcommunicates a fear of being judged.

Don't apologize for your shortcomings or failures. As with the previous point, just don't bring it up in the first place! Even if you really are tired, don't say so!

KEEP THE PRESENTATION MOVING FORWARD

Don't go backwards at the prospect's request. If you're at a certain point in the appointment and the prospect interrupts and asks to go back to a previous point, politely decline and say, "Let's continue moving forward, then we can revisit that after I'm finished." To let the prospect control the direction of the appointment and move it backwards not only hands your power to the prospect, but it also shows too much eagerness, as in, "I *really* need this sale!" Stick to your game plan and come back to it later.

ELICIT FEEDBACK TO FILL IN THE GAPS

You don't want to talk without feedback into a downward spiral. We all hate long, awkward pauses in a conversation, especially in a sales appointment. It's easy to get nervous about them and worry that the prospect has lost interest.

But filling in those gaps is the worst possible thing you can do. When you keep talking in order to fill in those gaps, you are subcommunicating insecurity and the fear that the prospect has lost interest. Make the prospect speak first and fill those gaps in.

TALK WITH SUFFICIENT VOCAL INTONATION AND INFLECTION

Have a lively voice! I've already mentioned that it's important to have powerful vocal projection and a voice that can be heard clearly; however, it's equally important to have vocal intonation and inflection. You don't want to bore your prospects to sleep with a monotonous voice that sounds like it's coming from a robot, so add some intonation and make your voice interesting and pleasant to listen to!

Those are the main points that you need to adhere to in order to avoid subcommunicating weakness and insecurity, which will of course cause you to lose all of your power when dealing with prospects.

For more on this topic, please visit NeverColdCall.com/Secrets, where you can access my complete 25-Point Power Checklist and learn more about the dynamics of power in selling.

5

TOP SALES PROS DON'T GO TO NETWORKING CLUBS

Do you go to networking events, chamber mixers, or leads clubs? If so, why? Why go to an event—one that you usually have to pay for, to boot—where you are in a room full of competitors and other sales reps, instead of decision makers? What is the benefit of that?

Here's something to think about. It's been several years since I've been to a chamber mixer or networking event. When I was still in sales and did attend an event, it was usually just for fun and for social reasons. Once I'd figured this out, I knew better than to expect any sales from it. However, I noticed something very profound when I went to those events, and I still notice it today on the rare occasion that I drop in on one to see old friends. The thing I notice is that all of the same people are still hanging out at those events—nothing has changed!

A friend of mine who is a very well-known Internet marketer has just, as I write this, released a report about the biggest problem facing the Internet marketing community: Specifically, Internet marketing is a relatively small, finite community, and it has reached the point where fewer and fewer people are making money because everyone in that small group is simply trying to sell Internet marketing products to each other. They've seen all the same sales tactics and marketing pitches over and over again. It's become incestuous.

The same is true with most networking events. If you go to all of the networking events held in any given city, you will find most of the same people at all of them. This was certainly the case for me, and for nearly every salesperson I've worked with. You show up at ABC event one week and meet everyone there. Then you go to XYZ event the following week, and all of the same people from last week are there. Go to another event another week, and you'll find the same group again.

Is it any wonder that no one makes any money at these events?

In my previous book, *Never Cold Call Again*, I told the story of how I was duped into applying for membership to a super-exclusive networking group, then arrived at my first meeting, only to find all the same jokers who wasted endless mornings at networking breakfasts and endless evenings at chamber mixers. I was furious that I had jumped through hoops to get into the group only to learn that it was a farce!

The biggest problem with networking events is that you'll rarely find any decision makers there—the people who can actually buy from you. They don't go, quite simply, because buying is easy! If people want to buy, they don't need to go to a networking mixer to meet people and find someone who is willing to let them buy. In other words, decision makers don't attend networking events, simply because buying is not difficult!

Selling, by contrast, is very difficult, and that's why salespeople who are stumped as to how to find leads and make sales continue to go to them with the dim hope that something will come of it.

If you want to benefit from networking, you've got to kick your networking up a notch or two. It's not going to help you to spend time in a room with other salespeople who are also out looking for leads. They can't help you. You must increase your status so that the people who *can* help you—the decision makers—will approach you and want to buy.

You can achieve this by offering to be the speaker at events. In any given city, there are at least a dozen or more networking events taking place each month, sponsored by chambers of commerce, neighborhood business communities, and many other entities. These events need speakers, and they don't have as easy a time finding them as you might think, simply because they have no budget to pay them. They need free speakers.

Remember the definition of persuasion, that it's the process of creating a win-win situation? Well, here's a huge win-win: They need speakers, and you need to kick your networking up a notch!

When you're the speaker at an event, rather than merely an attendee, your social status with that group goes through the roof. By that I'm not referring to snobbery or financial status; I simply mean taking the role of the leader. In any venue where there is a person speaking and others in the audience, the speaker automatically has higher status than the rest of the room and is looked up to as an expert for that reason. For example, in a classroom, the teacher has higher status than the students; the teacher is the leader.

You'll find that something very interesting takes place when you begin speaking at events, rather than showing up as an attendee. The decision makers who *are* present will approach you. Others who are in leadership roles—business and community leaders—will want to get to know you. You've just elevated your network, big-time. That makes it much, much easier to get the quality referrals that we all want and need in sales.

What can you speak about? Topics that are related to your industry, of course, featuring material from you that is strictly informational and helpful to any decision makers who may be in attendance. You'll establish yourself as a credible expert in your field by delivering that and keeping away from any sales pitches. You will, however, want to have business cards and/or fliers on hand complete with your Web address, and let everyone know you have a free e-mail newsletter available.

At NeverColdCall.com/Secrets, you'll find more great information and resources on how you can stop wasting time at fruitless networking events, and kick your networking up a few notches!

6

TOP SALES PROS GET HOT REFERRALS

Anyone who has been in sales for any length of time has been taught to do a good job, get the sale, and then come back and ask for three referrals. Anyone who has been in sales for any length of time has also been taught to cold call. "Do a good job and ask for three referrals" is usually just as effective as cold calling—meaning not at all.

I tried to "do a good job and ask for three referrals" for a long, long time. It didn't work. Sure, I got plenty of names from my customers, but the problem was that those names were simply not converting into sales. I needed to do something better.

There are a couple of different ways to approach the art and science of asking for referrals. First I'll tell you how I did it successfully, then I'll tell you a new method I've learned recently that's even better.

A few years into my sales career, I discovered that the company I was working for offered a paid referral program. Quite simply, whenever someone referred a lead to me that wound up buying, the referrer received a nice check in the mail a short time later. I began to pitch the referral program to the salespeople I had networked with, usually with little result, and signed them up for it.

Something amazing happened. Many of those same people who sat, half asleep, at the breakfast lead clubs, and who stood around at the chamber mixers looking bored and offering nothing, suddenly began introducing me to prospect after prospect, many of whom bought!

As I learned from Napoleon Hill, author of *Think and Grow Rich* (New York: Tarcher, 2005), you can never expect another person to do anything without adequate compensation. Providing networking partners and others with the possibility of earning commissions simply by referring people to you is the quickest and easiest way to begin getting a constant flow of hot referrals. It's especially powerful when you've just completed a sale, your new customer loves you because you've done all of the things a top sales pro does, and on top of it all you offer a financial incentive to send you referrals!

Referral fees are a basic part of Internet marketing. In fact, over 40 percent of all book sales on Amazon.com are the result of affiliates using their affiliate links to tell others about books—and, of course, those people earn commissions when the purchases take place. Why something that is so effective in the marketing world is so uncommon in the sales world is beyond me, but it is.

You have three options to get started on a referral program:

1. *Use a company-based referral program.* This is the best option because it's already in place, the money isn't coming out of your pocket, and you can get started immediately.
2. *If your company doesn't have one, suggest it.* I've had many of my clients do this, and the feedback I've received is that many companies are more than willing to set up a referral program if you simply approach them and explain how effective referral fees can be, and how you plan to use them to generate more sales.
3. *Offer referral fees out of your own commissions.* This option is less advantageous than the others, simply because the money is coming out of your own pocket. However, a percentage of something is always far better than nothing.

Here's an example. On my main web site, NeverColdCall .com, I run an affiliate program where people who sign up and then refer others to my web site earn a 50 percent commission on purchases made by people they referred. One of my products sells for $97. In scenario 1, someone is referred to my site, buys at $97, and I pay 50 percent commission to the referrer. I am left with $48.50. In scenario 2, that same person never hears about my site, never visits, and therefore never purchases, and I am left with exactly $0.

Naturally, I'd rather put $97 in my pocket than $48.50, but $48.50 is still infinitely better than $0! The same is true with your own commissions when you pay out a percentage for referrals, especially when you consider that simply having a qualified referral means that you're already halfway to the sale, and you didn't have to go through the effort of finding the lead in the first place.

Of course, a paid referral program isn't for everyone. For example, it is illegal for an insurance professional in the United States to pay a referral fee to anyone who isn't also a licensed insurance agent. That's why I offer you some other ideas on how to generate hot referrals without much effort, and without the useless advice of "Do a good job and ask for three referrals."

In my opinion, the hands-down best book on referral selling is Paul McCord's *Creating a Million-Dollar-a-Year Sales Income: Sales Success through Client Referrals* (Hoboken, NJ: John Wiley & Sons, 2007). That book explains a breakthrough method of getting referrals that is so effective, it's absolutely mind-blowing. Paul's system is based on rebuilding your entire sales process from the ground up, starting out by printing right on your business cards and marketing materials that you only work by referral. As I read the book, I realized that his approach not only sets up your prospects and customers to know in advance that they'll be expected to provide you with referrals, but it also makes you appear *extremely* successful!

Always remember that a top sales pro has the image of supreme success. Top sales pros go out of their way to display their success. You've undoubtedly seen "President's Club" in gold foil on business cards. This is done not to be arrogant, but because when a prospect sees that, they have an immediate desire to do business with that person. Success suggests that you are honest, have integrity, and are doing a superb job for your customers. People assume that you must be doing a great job for your clients, because if you weren't, how would you be able to rack up such impressive sales numbers? You wouldn't! Prospects assume that anyone who is dishonest or is not working hard for their clients would not be able to get more clients, due to a poor reputation and lack of referral business. That's why it's very important to have an image of success, and why top sales pros go out of their way to do so, including everything from their appearance and clothing to their business cards to their mannerisms and vocal tone.

When prospects see your business card and see the words, "Appointments by referral only," they will assume you must be so successful that you are fighting prospects off! Why else would you print that kind of qualifier on your card? They instantly assume that you are of the highest quality and integrity. Something else also gets triggered in their mind: the tendency of human nature to want what it can't have and to be put off by anything too easily available.

Think about how available the average salesperson is, and how quickly he'll rush out to anyone who wants to meet with him. Contrast that with a salesperson who has the words "Appointments by referral only" on his business cards. Very powerful.

Prospects will actually feel privileged to have the opportunity to meet and work with you. They'll feel fortunate to work with someone who is obviously the best in his field, and will be eager to entrust you with their business and their money. From that point forward, getting referrals from those prospects and customers becomes a natural part of the sales process. They'll know full well that you will expect referrals and that you deserve them.

For specific information and a referral selling tool kit, see Paul McCord's web site at PowerReferralSelling.com.

7

Top Sales Pros Are Competent Public Speakers

If you were to ask me what one thing has helped me more than anything else, both on my journey to becoming a top sales pro and in my overall career and life in general, I would have to say public speaking ability.

Back in 1999, the company I was working for required all of us to attend a weeklong public speaking class. I didn't want to go, for two reasons. First of all, a week in class meant a week out of the field. Sure, they reduced our quotas by 25 percent for that month—they always gave quota relief when mandatory training took place—but quota relief didn't replace the 25 percent of my commission check that would go missing thanks to lost selling time. Secondly, the last thing I wanted to do was to practice public speaking, especially after the first hour of the first day of that class when I learned that each of us would be required to get up and give a presentation in front of the room, every single day!

But that class turned out to be one of the most fun experiences of my life, and the best part is that it's still paying me big dividends today.

We were sent to that class because the company knew that public speaking ability translates into better sales ability, and that has certainly proven to be true. Remember when I mentioned the U.C.L.A. study that concluded that 93 percent of our communication is nonverbal, consisting of body language, vocal tone, and vocal presence? Well, while body language can be demonstrated and fairly easily learned, it takes a lot more practice to improve your vocal projection and intonation. Guess what the easiest way to do this is? You've got it—public speaking!

When you begin to learn public speaking skills, your voice automatically begins to improve. You speak with more clarity, more volume, more authority, and with much more confidence. You learn the proper intonation to make your voice sound interesting without sounding contrived. Your voice carries further, more easily, and you are heard clearly. Your posture and overall facial expression and body language improve as well, because they are all tied together, and anything that conveys confidence in one area automatically conveys more confidence in the others.

Here are some more benefits of acquiring public speaking skills, as they specifically relate to sales:

- Your prospects will hear you clearly and never ask you to repeat yourself.
- Your louder voice will enable you to practice better body language, such as leaning back when talking with prospects.

- You will learn how to get your point across with fewer words, thereby appearing more profound.
- Your speech will slow down to a level that creates the appearance of supreme confidence.
- You will begin to naturally add pauses to your speech, again creating the appearance of confidence, because pausing conveys that you know you have their interest and are not afraid of losing it.
- You'll practice better and more trustworthy eye contact with prospects.
- You will learn the proper posture and stance to make the best impression if you happen to make any presentations while on your feet.
- You'll learn how to move about in the most effective way when addressing multiple people.
- You'll learn how to divide your eye contact when addressing multiple people.

And there are more. As you can see, there is a lot to be gained from learning how to be a good public speaker. Like I said, that class several years ago has turned out to be one of the best investments of time I've ever made.

To learn these valuable skills yourself, you can look for a public speaking class—many community colleges and business training schools offer them—or you can join Toastmasters, the premier public speaking group in the world. You'll begin making presentations in front of groups, and get constructive criticism every time so you can continually improve until you become a top-notch speaker.

There is another huge benefit to having the ability to speak well that I haven't mentioned, and that's the benefit of increasing your status and your value in the eyes of your prospects and customers. When you speak at an event, whether it's big or small, you automatically establish yourself as the leader and the person with the highest status in that room. Decision makers who have the ability to buy from you will recognize this and will tend to seek you out. They will value your advice and opinions far more than they do those of average salespeople who do not put themselves in leadership positions by speaking publicly.

To get you started on the right track, here are some public speaking tips that will enable you to come across as a powerful, profound speaker:

- *Body language.* Body language is very important in public speaking. You want to have excellent posture, stand up straight, while also appearing relaxed—if you don't look relaxed, you'll come across as nervous. I like to stand straight while leaning back just slightly. Also, from time to time, I'll put one hand in my pocket while making gestures with the other. The audience perceives this as an indication of my ease and relaxation.
- *Movement.* It's important to move around, unless of course you're stuck talking into a fixed microphone, as will sometimes be the case. But if possible, move around. You'll notice that the best speakers are active on stage and rarely stand in one place for too long, because doing so bores an audience. I was taught to use the letter W to move around on stage. Imagine a big W painted on the stage, and walk along its lines from point to point as you

speak. I do this and it works very well for me. Such controlled movement conveys confidence and keeps the audience interested.

- *Vocal projection.* Practice speaking loudly but clearly. Powerful speech comes from your diaphragm, not your throat. That's why military drill sergeants can yell all day in a very powerful, deep voice, yet never get tired. Speaking from your core rather than your throat does not wear out your throat or your voice. My public speaking voice is many times louder than my regular talking voice. This came with practice and as a result of deliberately speaking from my core.

- *Eye contact.* It's important to make eye contact with members of your audience. If you simply glance around the audience, not making direct contact with any of the members, you'll come across as disconnected. A good general rule is to make eye contact with an audience member for three seconds, then disconnect, wait a short while, and then make eye contact with another audience member for three seconds. Continue this process throughout your presentation. You'll notice that people with whom you make eye contact suddenly sit up straight and pay attention because it's such a change from what they're used to—speakers who aren't all that great and who don't do this.

- *Humor.* Use humor sparingly throughout your presentation. This keeps people alert and interested. The mere act of laughing will step up your audience's attention level and keep them awake throughout the entire talk. When I say humor, I don't necessarily mean you should crack jokes; in fact, you probably should not in most cases. What

I'm referring to is something that makes people laugh and hopefully also gets a point across. For example, as a lead-in to the topic of the importance of a salesperson's control over an appointment, I ask everyone to stand up, look to their left, look to their right, and then sit back down. I then say, "There was no purpose at all to that, except to introduce my next topic: Top sales pros are in control!" This always gets a hearty laugh from everyone in the room and is a perfect lead-in to that part of my seminar.

- *Notes.* While you certainly should have notes so you don't forget any parts of your presentation, do not read from notes. I've seen speakers who will use a PowerPoint show as part of their presentation, and then simply read from it. Obviously, one could just distribute the PowerPoint to the audience members and skip the speech. While I do use PowerPoint presentations most of the time, I don't read from them verbatim. I use each slide to introduce a new topic or to reinforce a point, but I don't read it to the audience. The same is true with your notes—do not read from them. The purpose of notes is to outline all of your major points, to keep you on track during your talk, and to make sure you don't forget anything.

- *Pause.* I've talked about the power of inserting deliberate pauses while talking with prospects. The same is true while speaking to a group. Pauses are excellent for making points, getting people to think, and making you appear more confident and profound. Insert pauses frequently throughout your talk.

- *Handouts.* I don't like to give a handout to the audience until after my presentation. If they get it earlier, people tend to read through the handout instead of paying attention to me. I prefer to have a handout that outlines my presentation, printed copies of the PowerPoint slides I used, or both, available for everyone to take home, *after* my presentation is complete.

Those are the basics; however, knowledge of the basics can't replace actual experience, and the best place to start getting that experience is in Toastmasters or in a public speaking class where you'll be required to make presentations on a regular basis.

The ability to speak well in front of a group is a skill that no top sales pro is without. It definitely put me on the fast track to becoming a top sales pro and it will do the same for you. For more tips on public speaking, including a video in which I show you the basics, please visit NeverColdCall.com/Secrets.

8

TOP SALES PROS THINK LIKE BUSINESS OWNERS

If there's one thing that drives me crazy as a business owner, it's having to put up with salespeople who come in here trying to give me advice to "help" my business, but who obviously don't have any idea what they're talking about.

Here's a great example: I can't tell you how many times a salesperson has given their presentation, gotten to the price, heard me object and try to negotiate it down, and then said, "Well, that price isn't so bad when you consider the fact that it's a tax write-off." That line makes my blood boil.

It makes my blood boil because nearly every single business expense is a tax deduction! If I make a purchase for my business that is going to be used in my business, it's tax-deductible. Period. And don't even get me started on that term, *write-off*. It's totally inaccurate and I hate when people use it.

Salespeople are constantly walking into businesses, making claims that they can help, and then completely destroying their credibility by saying foolish things like, "This purchase is a tax write-off." It makes me realize that one of the key things salespeople must do to become top sales pros is to learn how a business works, and to start thinking like a business owner.

In sales, we've all been told that, in a way, we have our own business. After all, the sales profession provides a lot of freedom, the flexibility to create our own schedules, and, of course, the fact that our on-the-job performance directly impacts our income. If we produce, we make money. If we don't produce, we don't make money. Plain and simple. When you consider all of these reasons, it really is true—to an extent—that being in sales is like owning your own business.

The problems begin, however, when salespeople take that idea too far. It's one thing to control your own destiny through a sales position, but something quite different to run an actual business. A whole lot more goes into that effort, things that very few salespeople have any clue about at all.

The tax-deduction example is a great one because it's one I hear all the time, and because I've heard salespeople who I worked with using it, too. There are others, such as:

- "We can help your business."
- "This product will make your life easier."
- "We can help to improve your productivity."
- "We can save you money."
- "When you implement this, your efficiency will go up."

Every time a business owner or C-level decision maker hears statements like that, one question stands out in their minds:

"*How?*" And, sometimes, on top of that, they'll ask (to themselves), "Why do you think I care?"

The problem with trying to act like a business owner and speak a business owner's language when you've never actually been one is that you are speaking in terms of your own reality, and what concerns you would have in your world. You're unable to communicate in the same terms and about the key issues that a business owner is seriously concerned about.

There are only a handful of things any business owner even remotely cares about. These same key points hold true in consumer sales, as well—it's just a matter of positioning them appropriately. The three key business goals are as follows.

INCREASE REVENUES

Every sane business owner has one goal above all others, and that's to make more money. The easiest way to make more money is to bring in more revenues. In other words, more dollars coming in through the front door generally translate to more dollars in the bottom line and, ultimately, in the owner's pocket.

Some ways to increase revenues are:

- Increasing sales.
- Increasing conversion rate—the percentage of prospects who become customers.
- Getting customers to recommend us to others—viral marketing.
- Increasing the dollar value of each sale.
- Speeding up the sales process, thereby selling more product with the same number of staff.

- Getting continued, repeated sales from existing customers.
- Generating recurring revenue from customers—continuity products.

By the way, just glancing at this list will make you realize just how important the job of a salesperson is. Practically everything a company can do to increase revenues revolves around sales!

DECREASE EXPENSES

This is the simplest one on the surface, but be careful. Of course a company can put more money into its bottom line by cutting costs and saving money, but the problem is that cutting costs frequently cuts revenues as well. In a business, many expenses are actually investments that produce a positive return on investment (ROI). For example, the money I spend on advertising and marketing multiplies and comes back to me in a greater amount due to the sales it generates. My expensive Mac computer, which seems overpriced on the surface, makes me a lot more money than it cost, thanks to its superior podcasting, audio, and video production capabilities. It allows me to create and produce the CD and DVD courses I sell online and at live events. The fees I pay every month for my Web hosting server and Internet access make money for me because without them, I'd have no online sales. And so on, and so on.

Business owners cringe when they hear the words, "We can save you money," because a smart business owner will immediately begin to wonder how your cost-cutting ideas will turn into revenue-cutting nightmares. I just mentioned my Web server. What if I switched to another service that could provide me with hosting for my web sites at a lower cost, but it turned out to be less reliable? A few hours of downtime could quickly turn into hundreds of dollars in lost revenues. What if I had decided to save money by purchasing a less expensive computer? Buying something less expensive is always nice—we all like to have extra cash left over—but I couldn't create the multimedia and video I can with mine, which quickly generates far more money than any computer costs.

Now you understand why the words, "We can save you money," may very well be the *last* words you want to state to a business owner!

There's another big problem with trying to sell on price. If you set that precedent, and put the decision maker into a mind-set of buying on price and saving money, you're going to be in very big trouble when a cheaper alternative to you comes along. Remember, no matter how good you think your pricing is, someone else is always cheaper. If you live by price, you die by price.

Having said all that, cutting costs doesn't always mean buying a cheaper product. I cut my shipping costs by actually switching to a *more expensive* shipping company. It doesn't make much sense at first glance, but the cheaper company I was using lost too many packages before delivery, which meant that I had to ship a replacement. Not only did I wind up paying shipping twice, but I paid the cost of goods twice as well! By paying a little extra for shipping, I actually saved money in the end by avoiding the costs of shipping the same product to the same customer twice.

That example is also a good illustration of why business

owners cringe at the sound of a salesperson pitching a low price. It creates an expectation for the same quality of service I received from the inexpensive shipping company.

Ways to decrease expenses include:

- The obvious one: replacing something with a less expensive alternative.
- Switching to a better provider to reduce costly problems, even if that provider is more expensive, such as in my shipping example.
- Automating tasks rather than hiring employees to do them—this is a big one in the technology world.
- Finding a less expensive way to do the same thing, such as selling products via a web site rather than a retail store.

INCREASE EFFICIENCY

Increased efficiency allows a business to produce more, and therefore increase revenues, without figuring money into the equation. In other words, to increase the bottom line, a business typically either spends more money on something that generates a positive ROI, like advertising, or it finds ways to cut costs. By increasing efficiency, a business can increase revenues while neither increasing nor decreasing expenses.

As an example of something I've done to increase my efficiency, I have an assistant. She handles a lot of the tasks that I always did but didn't really need to. She screens my phone calls and e-mails, handles my schedule, deals with service providers, and so on. This leaves my time free to do things that move the business forward, rather than merely keep it operating at the same pace. For example, if I can write two books in the same amount of time it previously took me to write one, I've increased my efficiency and will make more money as a result. Having a personal assistant makes this possible.

Another example is that I recently hired a top marketing copywriter to rewrite my main web site. While I could have done that myself, having a professional do it offers two advantages: (1) A professional can do it better than I can, and (2) it again frees up my time to do work that I need to get done—say, for instance, writing this book! Since there are only so many hours in the day, and knowing that this book was a higher priority for me than rewriting the site, the site very well may have never gotten redone had I not hired the job out.

Efficiency is what allows a business to grow, to evolve. Most of us have been taught to ask irrelevant questions in appointments, like "Where do you want to be in five years?" The reality is that such a question really is important to a business owner. The problem is that we're taught to use it in the wrong context. Rather than asking it as a direct question, you need to do what top sales pros do, and that is to present yourself from the start as someone who is on a level playing field with business owners and who knows their challenges and responsibilities.

When you're able to walk into a business with the knowledge of what they really care about accomplishing, you can start having those discussions with business owners about the future and find them eager to talk with you, instead of asking random questions that are irrelevant and make you look like an amateur.

Some ways to increase efficiency are:

- Accomplishing the same task in less time—speeding up processes.
- Accomplishing more tasks in the same or less time—multitasking.

- Producing more quantity of product in the same amount of time.

- Hiring/outsourcing professional services: accountants, lawyers, consultants.

- Using personal services: hiring out tasks to save one's time.

- Instituting faster methods of payment, resulting in increased cash flow.

Having gone through the three key goals of any business, let's now revisit the issues I mentioned earlier—the claims that salespeople make without knowing quite why—and see how they are interpreted by a business owner:

- "We can help your business." Business owner thinks: "How? How can you help me? Be specific. Tell me, specifically, how you will be able to help me achieve one of the three key business goals."

- "This product will make your life easier." Business owner thinks: "How? And what makes you think I even care about that? I have three goals I need to achieve here to make my business successful, and only three, and that is not one of them. Will it make my business more efficient? If so, tell me exactly how. If not, get out of here. I don't need you."

- "We can help to improve your productivity." Business owner thinks: "Okay, you may have me interested but I need to know more, and you need to be specific. Are you going to increase my efficiency? If so, how?"

- "We can save you money." Business owner thinks: "Oh great, another one of these. This is the tenth salesperson

who has said that to me this week. And why would I want
to save money? To get a cut-rate provider who is going to
fail to come through when I really need them? No
thanks."

- "When you implement this, your efficiency will go up."
Business owner thinks: "Efficiency is good. How can you
increase my efficiency? Be specific—numbers talk and
something else walks."

The point here is that you need to avoid language that is
vague and that does not speak directly to one of the three key
business goals. When you do address one of those key goals,
you need to be specific. Know enough about the company in
advance to speak intelligently to the owner, enough so that
they will be interested enough in hearing more—and hopefully wanting to *buy* from you!

One thing that business owners love to hear is concrete
numbers and especially hard dollars. For example, one of the
methods of advertising that I use consistently brings me a 400
percent ROI. In other words, for every dollar I put into it, I get
four dollars back. Naturally, I spend as much with that company as I possibly can each and every month.

However, I've never seen this particular company promote
its marketing program with any specific numbers, case studies,
or concrete results. I'm sure a lot of business owners would
give their full, undivided attention to any advertising medium
that can show case studies with 400 percent returns on investment. However, they talk in vague terms, such as "Advertise
your business fast and easy, and effectively—your message will
be in front of our entire audience," and so on. Most business

owners yawn at those types of messages unless there are concrete numbers involved.

It's also important to remember that successful people value their time above all other assets. Showing business owners how to save time is almost as good as handing them cash—maybe better, depending on what the person's time is worth. When I pay others to do tasks instead of doing them myself, it's because having them do them saves me time. Time is money, and I can then use that time to do things that will make more money and move the business forward, rather than using my time to do mundane tasks that I could outsource. The same is true for every business owner. If you can show them how to recover even a little bit of time every day, they'll be grateful and they'll respect you for it.

Now that you understand the three key business goals—increase revenues, decrease expenses, and increase efficiency—let's put everything together, because when you do that, you arrive at the ultimate language of the business owner: *profit justification*.

Most of us have heard or even used the term *cost justification* at some time or another. Cost justification is simply the concept that the product will pay for itself over time. However, that's not good enough for most savvy business owners. They want to *make* money, not *recover* it. They want to increase their investment—create a positive ROI—not just break even. Who wants to break even? Smart business owners don't—they want to come out ahead. When you profit-justify your solutions, you show prospects how your products will actually *make money* for them.

I use my high-end computer as an example. It makes money

for me. It is capable of creating products that I can sell at a significant profit margin. The same is true with my video and lighting equipment. That wasn't purchased for the sake of breaking even. It was purchased with the intent of making money, and it does.

Even the high-end suits I wore as a salesperson were profit-justified. They increased my sales thanks to the great impression they made on prospects and, more importantly, the increased confidence I gained by wearing them every day. Every time I bought one, I pictured myself as a very successful person, well-dressed and making tons of sales.

When I make purchases for my business, I don't look for toys that will pay for themselves over time. I look for money-makers. So do all other business owners.

Profit-justifying a solution isn't difficult at all, as long as you understand how business owners think and you know the right questions to ask to get them thinking that way with you. Let's say, for instance, that I don't have the computer and video equipment to create DVDs and you are trying to sell it to me. The conversation might go something like this:

You: "Frank, when we discussed your sources of revenue, you mentioned that you had considered the possibility of offering a monthly subscription product, is that correct?"

Me: "Yes, most likely a CD series as many other marketers provide."

You: "And what price do you imagine you could charge for that?"

Me: "For an audio CD? Oh, I'd imagine about twenty dollars per month."

You: "Well, how can you increase that price? Obviously, it would be difficult to get people to pay much more than twenty dollars for a one-hour CD. What if you could offer something more, say a video DVD? People are willing to pay much more for a DVD than a CD, especially in the sales training world."

Me: "That's correct, and I've already thought about it. I could possibly charge fifty dollars per month for a DVD series. However, an audio CD is easy to create with my current computers, and I'm not video-capable. And having to go to a studio once a month is not only a hassle, but it would be prohibitively expensive. I'd have to charge a hundred dollars for each DVD for that to make sense. That's why I'm sticking to CDs. They're easy to create on a computer."

You: "Frank, video isn't hard. In fact you may find that putting together a DVD is just as easy as a CD when you have the right equipment and software for it."

Me: "I had no idea. I thought only professional studios could do that. Tell me more."

You: "Let's meet again next week—I'll put something together for you. By the way, how many subscribers do you anticipate for your product?"

Me: "It's hard to give a concrete number without actually making the product available, but based on my knowledge of my customer base, the worst-case scenario would be five hundred subscribers."

A week later, we meet again. You come back with a software demonstration on your laptop that shows me just how simple it is to create DVDs. I'm impressed and get excited about moving my business forward into a new realm, video!

Me: "Okay, I'm excited, but what is all this going to cost me?"

You: "What I did before coming here was to put together some numbers for you. Based on your worst-case scenario of five hundred subscribers, I calculated what your income would be for both a CD and a DVD series at the prices we discussed."

Audio CD Series

Monthly subscription price	$ 20
× 500 subscribers	$ 10,000
Less cost of goods sold	(1,000)
Monthly profit	$ 9,000

DVD Video Series

Monthly subscription price	$50
× 500 subscribers	$ 25,000
Less cost of goods sold	(2,500)
Monthly profit	$ 22,500
Cost of video setup—computer, camera, lighting, and miscellaneous equipment	(20,000)
Profit generated in first month	$ 2,500
Profit generated in first year	$250,000

You: "Frank, this $20,000 investment in equipment, which may seem steep at first, is going to generate a profit for you the very first month! And it will add up to a very large profit over the course of the first year, and every year thereafter."

Me: "Wow! This is really amazing. You're right, I wouldn't spend that kind of money to have a video studio for fun, but looking at these numbers, I don't see how I could do without one in my business. How soon can you deliver this and get it installed?"

That example is classic profit justification. And, as you can see, you didn't even have to close me. There was no real selling involved. Once I saw your profit justification figures, I was practically begging you to let me buy!

Profit justification is clearly the most powerful tool any salesperson can have when working with a business owner. It's the language of the business owner, and for that reason, it's the language of the top sales pro.

What I've talked about thus far is just a glimpse of the knowledge that a top sales pro has when it comes to understanding how a business owner thinks. There is a lot more to it than that, but hopefully this chapter has given you a clear picture of what your thinking process must be when you're working with business owners, and where to start. While it's not necessary to start taking business finance and accounting courses, I strongly advise salespeople to read some basic books on business finance, accounting, and cash flow, in order to change your thinking from that of a salesperson to that of a business owner.

At NeverColdCall.com/Secrets you'll find more information on the triggers that make business owners buy, as well as real-life examples of successful profit justification.

9

TOP SALES PROS ARE RECOGNIZED EXPERTS

Few things will get you more sales and obliterate your competition faster than being perceived as a recognized expert. When you are perceived as a recognized expert in your field, you are no longer a salesperson as far as your prospect is concerned. You have just become a valuable consultant, a trusted business adviser. This is what all top sales pros are to their prospects and customers.

Imagine what it would be like to be a prospect who has a need and is naturally meeting with several different salespeople in order to compare their options and, of course, pricing. The first few salespeople come in and fit the stereotype of a typical salesperson. They are obviously in need of a sale and act like it, saying stupid things like, "What will it take to earn your business?" (Never ask that question, by the way.) They give their company story, talk about the clients they've served, claim to have the best customer service, ask the usual salesy questions that may or may not be relevant to the prospect's business, come back with a cookie-cutter proposal, and then try to get the sale with one or more pushy closing tactics.

Then you walk in. You're dressed very professionally and have an air of prosperity about you due to your exemplary body language and having followed my social dynamics checklist. You avoid useless small talk that would otherwise waste the prospect's time. Your speech is confident, clear, and succinct, thanks to your having gained some basic public speaking skills. Unlike the other salespeople, you appear to be very relaxed and stress-free, which the prospect immediately interprets to mean that you are already doing well and don't need to beg for his business. Your questioning process is totally relevant to the prospect's business, because it is intended to lead to a profit-justified proposal. In addition, your questioning process makes it clear to the prospect that you intend to give him a solution that legitimately helps him—which makes you take on the appearance of a *trusted business adviser*, not a salesperson.

At the conclusion of the appointment, after you've already thoroughly impressed your prospect and quietly convinced him that you are a person to whom he can entrust his business, you thank him for his time and hand him a few sheets of paper, stapled together. You say, "Here is some information about me and my credentials for you to review, because I want to make sure you know that you and your business will be in good hands with me. I look forward to meeting with you again."

The prospect then peruses the papers you've just handed

over, to find news stories and press releases quoting you as an expert in your field, along with one or more published articles that you've written.

You've just crushed any chance the competition had for getting that sale. You see, when you are *the* recognized expert in your field—and you can prove it with news stories and press items citing you as the expert—your prospects won't even consider doing business with anyone else.

The fact is that people who are quoted in the news as experts in their field are almost always very highly paid consultants whom most prospects cannot afford to hire. For example, marketing experts who are quoted in the news frequently charge up to $25,000 or more just to write a sales letter or Web page—just *one!* This is the case with top experts in any field. The lawyers who are quoted in the news as experts are also the most expensive. Authors like me who have been quoted in the news and who have had several articles published carry very high consulting fees.

People are willing to pay a lot—and I mean a *lot*—for an expert opinion that can help to improve their businesses or their lives. Then you come walking in, possessing the same or possibly even better credentials, and give them an opportunity to work with you for free. All they need to do is buy from you.

Are you now beginning to see why positioning yourself as an expert in your industry makes it so easy to get sales? Are you also beginning to see how simple it is to get people to *buy* from you, so that you'll never have to *sell* to them? Once you learn how to do business as I'm teaching you in these pages, you'll never have to close another sale. People will just buy.

When you are a recognized expert and you can back it up

with news stories and published articles, prospects forget about why they should or should not buy from you. They begin to consider the fact that you are a recognized expert who can potentially help them in really big ways, and instead of having to pay you astronomical consulting fees, all they have to do is buy from you! They know that, as your customer, they will have a guaranteed audience with you.

This is exactly why top sales pros are seen as recognized experts. Becoming a recognized expert is one of—if not the—most powerful things you can do to supercharge your sales career.

Now, I know what you're thinking—you're probably telling yourself that it's not so easy to get your name in the news, and as an expert in your field to boot. Nothing could be further from the truth. Here are three quick, easy, and very simple ways to become a recognized expert in your industry—a guru, if you will—and have the ability to back that claim, literally overnight.

ARTICLE MARKETING

One thing you can do right now that is absolutely free is to write one or more articles relevant to your industry and post them to article directories on the Internet. My personal favorite is EzineArticles.com.

I do this all the time, and it's a very big reason why I'm seen as an expert in the sales profession. It also drives tons of people to my web sites, where they wind up buying my products. That's why I use the term *article marketing* instead of just telling you to write articles. Your articles not only give you credibility as an expert, but they also bring you plenty of exposure, and lots of new prospects along with it. What's more, when people search online for information pertaining to your industry, your articles will begin to appear as they multiply and spread throughout the Internet.

And yes, believe me, they spread. The entire purpose of EzineArticles.com is to give web site owners and newsletter publishers a source of articles to include in their publications. That's why they're called *free reprint* articles—when you submit your article, you also give permission to others to reprint it for free. There is one catch though: Anyone who reprints your article is required to include the resource box at the bottom. A resource box is simply your bio. Here's how a good resource box might look at the end of one of your articles:

John Doe is a full-time Widget expert and marketer in Anytown, USA. To learn more, and to receive John's free Widget newsletter, please visit www.JohnsWidgetSite.com. You may also contact John directly at john@johnswidget site.com.

You can also upload a photo to appear in your resource box, alongside your bio.

I received an e-mail not too long ago from someone who had taken my advice. He wrote a few articles on his industry and uploaded them to EzineArticles.com. Three months later, his handful of articles appeared on over 500 web sites. At that point, he was receiving e-mails and inquiries every day from prospective customers who wanted to talk with him!

His effort in writing the articles only took a couple of hours, and three months later it began to pay off very handsomely. He now has a full funnel of qualified prospects who *want to buy* from him. Thanks to that, and to the referrals he is gaining from those people—who are all eager to tell their friends and colleagues that they are working with a published expert—and the constantly increasing exposure and credibility he's now getting from his articles, he'll probably never have to prospect again.

The benefits of article marketing, for salespeople, are three-fold. First, you gain exposure and begin to have prospects calling you because of it. Nearly all savvy prospects do their research on the Internet nowadays before making any purchasing decisions, so having your articles all over the Internet places you into a very strong position to be exposed to people who are in a current buying cycle, and to have them call you. Remember how the power dynamic works when a prospect calls you first? It's also very nice to work exclusively with prospects who are in a current buying cycle, rather than idle shoppers and people who won't be making a decision anytime in the near future.

Second, you're able to establish an amazingly high level of credibility with those prospects with whom you're already working. In the scenario at the beginning of this chapter, I mentioned handing your articles to a prospect at the conclusion of an appointment in order to solidify your expert credibility in their minds. That's one way to do it. Another great way is to e-mail (or snail mail) your articles to a prospect prior to a meeting. Instead of the usual, "Thank you for the opportunity to meet with you" letter, or the "I'm writing to confirm our appointment" letter, you can forward links to your articles, along with a brief note stating, "I look forward to meeting with you. Here are some recently published articles I've written that will hopefully familiarize you a bit more with what I do, so that I'll be better able to address your needs when we meet in person."

That not only establishes your credibility, but it also puts you in a very positive light, because you are talking about serving your prospect's needs instead of making a sale. It also reinforces your ability to maintain control over the entire sales process because, remember, the person who is in a position to fulfill a need has the power; the person who has a need to be fulfilled is not in power. You need power to get sales, and this is another way to get it and keep it.

Third, article marketing gets your name out there. It puts you into the category of an *Internet celebrity*, a term I'm hearing more and more these days.

Did you know that most savvy prospects today will Google your name? That's right. Before meeting with you, smart prospects will get online and run a search for your name—especially if you're in a personal services industry, such as real estate or insurance. (Make no mistake though—business prospects do this, too.) They're looking, first of all, for any negative publicity or complaints against you. But mostly, they're looking to find out who you are, or, more specifically, if you are anybody at all.

My client who used article marketing told me he had a major edge over his competition because, when people Google him, there are over 500 results for his name! That's because of the 500 sites that have picked up his articles, and there are more every week.

Once you've implemented article marketing into your overall sales strategy, it won't hurt to tell prospects to look you up online. Once you're on a large number of sites, you can modestly hand one or two articles to your prospect and say, "If you're interested in learning more, just search online under my name and you'll find more."

Try it! I just ran a Google search for "Frank Rumbauskas." There are over 20,000 results. The third one says "Frank Rumbauskas—EzineArticles.com Expert Author." You'll have the same thing showing up under searches for your name once you do this. Do it right now—the results will be there in a few days, and you'll have an article online, establishing you as an expert, ready to hand to your prospects *tomorrow*!

As a final note, I'll mention that there are plenty of free reprint article directories online besides EzineArticles.com. That one just happens to be my favorite. Search for others, and submit your articles to all of them! I'd also recommend writing articles on a fairly regular basis, such as once per month. That way you're constantly adding new content and gaining more exposure for yourself. It's also a good idea to send out a new article to your newsletter list every month, something I'll touch on in Chapter 11 and that I've covered extensively in my previous book, *Never Cold Call Again: Achieve Sales Greatness Without Cold Calling* (Hoboken, NJ: John Wiley & Sons, 2006).

PRESS RELEASES

Press releases are largely misunderstood, and for that reason they're practically unknown as a tool for salespeople. Even worse, salespeople assume that press releases are out of their reach, and as a result, they never even consider them. This is a major mistake, because press releases, when used properly—as I'm about to show you right now—are 10 times more powerful than the article marketing strategy I just explained!

You don't need to hire a public relations firm to take advantage of press releases. You don't need to have any reporter friends and you don't need to be famous. As with article marketing, everything you need is online. Personally, I like PRWeb.com and that's who I use for my own press releases. Unfortunately, this strategy isn't free like article marketing is. However, it's extraordinarily powerful, even more so than articles, and for that reason it's worth every penny! At the time of this writing, you can issue a press release to major media outlets for $80 on PRWeb.com. How many sales would it take to make up for that? Not many, I'm assuming. Take my advice and use press releases!

There are several reasons why press releases are so powerful. The biggest one, for me, is that your press release will automatically be included in Yahoo! News and Google News. That's huge—really huge. I don't know about you, but I browse Yahoo! News on a fairly regular basis. When I come across an interesting or important story, I click the "E-mail to a Friend" link and send it to my friends, who then get the story in their e-mail and can open it up and read it.

Guess what? When you issue your release, it's going to show up in Yahoo! News just like all the rest of the news stories that day! *You won't be able to tell the difference between your press release and the major news stories of the day.*

Think of how your prospects are going to see you when you can hand them a Yahoo! News story where you are quoted as an expert in your industry! Is there any doubt in your mind as to why this tactic leaves your competition with no chance, and firmly establishes you as a credible expert, a *trusted business adviser* with whom every prospect will want to entrust their business?

Not only can you print your news story and hand it to a prospect in person, you can also use the "E-mail to a Friend" link to send it to prospects when it comes out. I strongly advise you, on the day that your release is issued, to find the story in Yahoo! News and e-mail it to any and all prospects you've ever had, and to your customers, too! It's also a great idea to send it to powerful networking contacts, both those with whom you're already working and those whom you are trying to secure but who haven't paid much attention to you in the past.

Of course, your story will also be in Google News, so you can send it from there if you choose—it's your preference. And in addition to inclusion in Yahoo! News and Google News, you'll be able to download and print a nicely formatted pdf copy of your press release.

On top of all the news inclusion, press releases also work extremely well in getting your name out there in online search results. There are two big benefits to this. The first is that press releases and news stories tend to rank very high in search results, because search engines give preference to noncommercial Web pages—that is, pages that aren't selling anything. The second is that when prospects search for your name online, they're going to see you coming up as the focus of news stories!

Yahoo! News and Google News inclusion will prove to be very powerful in persuading prospects that you are the only logical choice for them to buy from. However, on top of that, if your release is interesting, significant, and well-written, it has a good chance of being picked up by other news outlets. For example, one of my releases was picked up and run by every CNN-affiliate station in the United States. Talk about serious coverage!

When I'm trying to make a purchasing decision, I'm going to go with the person who's been in the news, not someone who has no name at all, and therefore no credibility. And I believe the majority of prospects make decisions the same way.

What to write in your press release? This is important, because a press release that is an obvious sales pitch is not going to be picked up by anyone. What you want to accomplish in a press release is to convey some bit of information about your industry, quote you as an expert in your industry, and do it all in a way that is interesting and newsworthy, not salesy. Here's the press release I issued via PRWeb.com for a mere $80 that was picked up by all those CNN-affiliate stations:

COLD CALLING DISAPPEARING FROM SALES TACTICS:
TECH-SAVVY MARKETERS KNOW WHAT DOESN'T WORK

Phoenix, AZ (PRWEB)—Cold calling is going away. That's the word from Frank Rumbauskas, an author and sales trainer on the subject.

"Cold calling was always a rite of passage in sales. Now that's all changed, and this generation of sales professionals isn't buying it. They can see why cold calling doesn't work and they don't want to fall into that trap," said Rumbauskas.

He went on to explain that people are so sick and tired of receiving cold calls that they respond with anger and frustration, and new salespeople don't want to deal with that.

Also, today's sales rookies are very Internet-savvy and marketing-savvy and know that cold calling is the least effective of their options.

"New entrants to sales try cold calling, but when they see how infuriated their prospects become, they either drop it or change careers," Rumbauskas said.

He went on to say, "Now with the evolution of online business networking sites that have tens of millions of members, salespeople have a simple way to make tons of great connections, which makes cold calling even less useful. The Internet has really changed the way this new generation of salespeople approach their jobs."

Rumbauskas explained that the bottom line is that cold calling is dead in today's world, and is a relic of a previous generation. Today's top producers are using self-marketing to get ahead quickly.

See? Nothing fancy! That release was short, sweet, and to the point, and that's exactly why it was picked up by major media outlets.

Remember, when writing your release, make it newsworthy. Think of something that will interest people. Obviously, the idea that cold calling is dead isn't breaking news and is nothing new, but because it was couched in the format of a news story, with a news-appropriate headline, it was appropriate to be run in the news.

By the way, your release needn't be as short as mine. However, I wouldn't recommend going over 500 words, as that may be considered too lengthy and hurt your chances of having it picked up. Having said that, though, it's going to run in Yahoo! News and Google News regardless, and that's reason enough to make the press release strategy more than worth your time and money.

NEWS QUERY SERVICES

This third way to become a recognized expert is both the most expensive and the least guaranteed to work. However, when it does work, the results are so spectacular—better than article marketing and press releases put together—that I've chosen to include it here. It's not for everyone, but if you're willing to make the investment of time and money, follow through with it, and be patient, you'll be glad you did.

News query services are where reporters go when they need to find experts to help them with a news story. Here's how it works, using myself as an example. A reporter doing a story on sales will put out a query to sales experts. The query includes the topic of the article, the specific kind of information the reporter needs, and the reporter's contact information (think of it as a sort of reverse press release).

As a subscriber to the query service, I've indicated that I'd like to receive all queries relating to sales and marketing stories, and as a result I receive an e-mail a short while later containing the details of the query. If it's for a story that I feel I'm qualified to comment on, I'll send an e-mail to the reporter giving one or two sentences of background information about myself and who I am, followed by responses to the specific questions in the query. The reporter then reads all of the responses he's received and chooses one or more to include in the story.

When you read an article in a magazine or newspaper and see a quote from an expert, 99 percent of the time that quote was obtained in the method I've just described. However, to a reader, it appears that the reporter actually spoke with and interviewed the expert, which gives the story a lot more weight and a more personal feel.

As I mentioned, this is not guaranteed to work, and it requires a lot of patience. You're not going to receive queries for your particular area of expertise every day—I get only a few a month—and you're ultimately at the whim of the reporter, who has the final say as to whether you'll be included in the story. However, when this tactic pays off, it can pay off big. Not only will it give you a level of expert credibility that cannot be obtained any other way, but it can also open doors for you and really elevate your career in a way that nothing else can. These stories are typically for major magazines and other high-visibility publications.

The query service I use is PRLeads.com. At the time of this writing, the cost is $99 per month. It's not cheap, but think of what can happen to your sales and your career if you are quoted as an expert in a major publication with tons of visibility. The potential results are nothing to sneeze at!

As you can see, it's a fast and simple process to establish yourself as a recognized expert, and the results are tremendous! I think it's sheer insanity for any salesperson not to do these things, especially the first two, and yet only a tiny handful do!

Once you begin to use these tactics, I highly recommend putting together a media kit, and always having a few on hand in your car or briefcase. A media kit is nothing fancy—it's simply a presentation folder, the kind most of us use for proposals, containing a couple of your articles and press releases, and, if you've been fortunate enough to succeed with the third tactic I explained, reprints of magazine articles featuring you. Put a couple of business cards in there, too—I like the folders with a business card cutout inside.

If you want to get really fancy, or if you're in a high-end market where your big commissions will justify the cost, have a professional photo taken and have custom folders made with your name, photograph, and contact information printed on the front cover.

I use media kits myself. It's the standard method that professional speakers use to make themselves known to meeting planners and others who are in need of our services. Guess what's included in my media kit? You guessed it—among other things, like a demo DVD, are my press releases, news stories, and an article or two!

Give your media kit to prospects. Have it available in all networking situations, especially those where you're speaking, as you should be. That reminds me—sending out a media kit is a very easy way to secure those free speaking opportunities I mentioned in Chapter 5. If you call or e-mail a chamber of commerce association and simply offer your speaking services, they won't take you nearly as seriously as if you mail them a media kit showing your expert credentials. You might even get offers for *paid* speaking gigs if you do that!

If you use only one chapter in this entire book, use this one. It will make you a top sales pro instantly. Put this book down right now. Write and submit your first article. Write and submit your first press release. If you do those two things today, you'll have expert credibility tomorrow—literally! Remember, knowledge without action is dead, so use this knowledge right now.

By the way, your expert status gained through publishing articles and press releases is very powerful in career advancement. Next time you're up for a promotion or pay raise, or when you have an annual review, bring your media kit along with you. It will make a profound impact and enable you to ask for and get much more than you could otherwise. The same is true for job interviews, and for small business owners seeking loans and/or investors. And, like I said, get enough coverage and doors will begin to open up to you that you never knew existed!

For even more information on getting yourself established as a recognized expert, please see NeverColdCall.com/Secrets, where you'll also find sample articles and press releases, as well as my own media kit for your reference.

10

Top Sales Pros
Get and
Use Free PR

In Chapter 9, I showed you how to establish yourself as a recognized expert in your field in order to get more prospects calling you and to easily close more sales due to your desirability as a trusted business adviser. In this chapter, I show you how to use your newfound expert status to get local media coverage that will generate a ton of leads for you and further solidify your status as a guru in your industry. It will also get people to contact you, ready and wanting to buy. This is another step toward never selling again.

When I explained the news query services that reporters use to find sources for stories, you may have been wondering why reporters would need to use those services to begin with. After all, aren't they inundated with people and public relations firms vying for their attention? Don't they have hundreds, if not thousands of people knocking on their doors, trying to get media coverage?

No. As I've mentioned in my previous books, reporters have to prospect, too! They are under constant pressure and endless deadlines to always come up with new and interesting stories to write and print. It's hard for most people to realize, but coming up with fresh material on an ongoing basis is far more difficult than it sounds.

In addition, reporters don't have a barrage of people asking for coverage because most people don't think they'll actually get it. It's similar to how the most attractive people complain that they can't get any dates—other singles are too intimidated to approach them. The same is true with the media. Few people think they'll be granted a story or an interview, so they don't even bother trying.

I'm willing to guess that you, too, have assumed that media coverage is out of your reach, and that only those on a very high level have access to it. But nothing could be further from the truth. By making yourself known and available to reporters as a source for a new story, you provide them a very valuable service. Yours is one less story they'll have to come up with on their own. And with the recognized expert status you'll now have, thanks to the tactics and techniques I explained in Chapter 9, getting reporters to talk to you will be a piece of cake.

The first thing you'll need to do is to create a list of media you'd like to target. I recommend starting with local newspapers, community and/or business park publications, and business journals. My best results came from stories that ran in business journals, because I happened to be in business-to-business sales. What media you choose to target may depend on what it is you're selling, and to whom.

To find the reporters you'll need to contact, get a copy of each of the publications and find stories about topics and industries that might be similar to yours. Each reporter for a particular publication focuses on a specific area of expertise, so you'll need to find out who those reporters are. Obviously, their names are printed along with the articles. Many publications also print their telephone numbers and/or e-mail addresses. If they don't, simply visit the publication's web site, or call their main number to get that information.

Speaking of web sites, in many cases you won't even have to obtain copies of the publications you'd like to target because they have online versions that you can access for free, or because all of the reporters' names and their specialties are published on the site.

Once you've implemented the techniques from Chapter 9, you'll have your media kit together. Media kits are industry standard with media outlets—hence the term—and are seen as professional by reporters. This is the first step toward getting media coverage. Send a media kit out to each of the reporters you are targeting, along with a cover letter that introduces you, states that you are an expert in whatever your particular industry is, and mentions that several articles by you and news stories quoting you are enclosed. Let the reporter know that you'll be following up shortly. (In many cases, they'll call you first if they are on deadline for a new story and happen to like what they see in your media kit.)

After all of your media kits are sent out, wait a few days, and then go ahead and call or e-mail each individual reporter. I like to offer to take them out to lunch to introduce myself and to discuss what's newsworthy in my industry. Most will take you up on your offer after they see that you do have expert status and may be able to contribute something of value to them. You'll find that most reporters will be willing, if not eager, to meet with you and to do a story.

Be sure to have the reporter include your contact information in the story. They'll rarely print a telephone number, but most will happily include your Web address as they know that many readers will want it. You'll learn the whys and hows of having your own personal web site in Chapter 11, but for now I simply want you to realize how important it is to have your *own* means of contact, including your own web site.

BE YOUR OWN AGENCY

Remember when I explained that being in sales actually is, in some ways, similar to owning your own business? As you implement what you learn in this book, you'll definitely transform into a top sales pro, and as part of that transformation, you'll need to create your own company of sorts—at least some of the basic infrastructure of one.

From this point forward, no matter what company you work for, I want you to think of yourself not as an employee but as an agency. You are your own company, a sales agency representing the company whose products or services you sell.

Naturally, every sales agency needs some basic infrastructure—a telephone number, an e-mail address, a fax number, and a web site. These are the things you need for your agency, and they will be *yours* and yours alone. Why? When you become a respected expert in your field, you are doing so for yourself as a person, not for your company. When you get media coverage, you're doing it to advance yourself and your expert status, not your company's. Remember, prospects are going to want to do business with you, very much so, because of *your* expert status, regardless of where you work or where you may go in the future.

Because this book is all about making *you* a top sales pro, as you create this image of power and expert status and generate great numbers of leads with it, you'll want to make sure all of the contact information you use is portable—your own.

There are two reasons for this. The first is a subject I don't like to bring up, but it happened to me—a lot—and I'd be willing to bet that it goes on in many sales offices. That's the problem of having other salespeople in the office who have sticky fingers and who will want to steal your leads. In my previous book, *Never Cold Call Again*, I explain the basics of creating marketing pieces to generate leads, and the importance of printing a fax-back response form on those pieces. I recommend getting your own fax number to do this, and here's why.

When I began using direct mail and flier distribution services, I found that including a fax-back form on the piece more than tripled response rates (a fax-back form is simply a space where prospects can fill in their name and phone number and fax it to you). However, I initially had the office fax number printed on those marketing pieces. I quickly learned that if I was not physically present in the office when those fax-back forms came in, I usually would not get them. Someone else would see it, grab it, call the prospect, and get the sale, thanks to all of my hard work. That's reason number one as to why I recommend having your own personal contact information.

It's accessible to you and only you, and dishonest co-workers won't be able to steal your leads.

The second reason I recommend having your own contact information, which includes phone number, fax number, e-mail, and web site, is because if you switch jobs, and the office numbers and web site for your previous company are on your materials, you'll have to start from zero all over again when you make the change. That is totally unnecessary. You'll want to continue building on what you've already accomplished if you ever make a change of employer. Remember, I want you to think of yourself as your own sales agency. Your employer merely provides the products you sell and pays you commission—a fee for services, if you will, for selling those products.

This is all about moving yourself up to the level of a top sales pro. You can't do that if you find yourself left with nothing, back to square one, if you change jobs. So make sure that the means available for prospects to contact you is portable. There's no point in going through all of this effort to achieve greatness, only to have your successors loot your hard work when you move on.

Don't doubt the importance of this. It's been four years now since I've left active sales to become an author and speaker, and to this day I still get calls from people looking to buy the product I was selling four years ago! There's a powerful cumulative effect to my strategies, and they are very long lasting, so keep that in mind as you build and use them.

Your web site will be the primary means of contact for people who see your news coverage and decide to contact you. So make sure it's included in all of the news stories that are run about you.

BUILDING LEGITIMACY

When I obtained coverage in my local business journal, the number of leads I got was staggering. I was able to get two more stories run by that same reporter for that same business journal, and I encourage you to do the same. It doesn't take long for reporters to run out of ideas and material. They'll be happy to hear from you again and to do another story on a different area of your expertise, or simply to report a different angle on your first story.

After I'd gotten those business journal stories run, I approached a local suburban newspaper with those clippings and easily got a story printed there, this time with a photo included. Again, the results were staggering, and I had plenty of people contacting me, requesting appointments. They saw me as the expert and wanted to buy from me so they'd get the added benefit of having me on their side as a trusted business adviser.

You see, there's a very important element to news coverage that you may not realize, and it is applicable to the press release strategy as well. That's the power of *legitimacy*. When people read through a newspaper, they see the ads and interpret them as such. However, people interpret news stories as fact. If it's a news story, people believe, then it must be true. It's well known that one news story is worth more than thousands of dollars of expensive advertising, because a news story is so much more effective.

The irony here is that 80 percent of all news stories are placed! They become news as a result of what you're learning here—reporters approach experts and vice versa, and, of course, those experts have positioned themselves as experts simply to get media coverage, just as you're going to do. (I've read that nearly all of the remaining 20 percent of news coverage is biased or spun to reflect the reporter's and/or publication's opinion. Very interesting.)

After you've succeeded in getting news coverage, guess what you're going to do next? You've got it—clip those stories and add them to your media kit! (Be careful with making copies here—many papers that claim copyrights on their stories will require you to pay a fee, or to buy reprints from them, if you wish to distribute them.) As you add more stories to your media kit, it will become more powerful and will therefore make it easier and easier for you to continue to get more coverage. You'll have reporters from other publications calling you, because they are very competitive, read each other's papers, and don't want to be left out when a new story breaks.

You'll also be able to kick your level of media coverage up a notch. Several of my clients have obtained appearances and interviews on local radio shows after getting their names in print. A few have even made it onto television! I'm sure you've noticed that local businesspeople are frequently featured or spotlighted on your local morning news shows. Guess what? You can be, too! Once you've got a few articles, press releases, and now some news stories in your media kit, it won't be too difficult to approach local television stations. You may find that getting on the local morning news show is easier than you thought it would be—you certainly don't have to hire an overpriced PR firm to do this for you.

One bit of advice about television interviews: The studio waiting rooms for guests are well stocked with coffee, tea, water, soda, and other goodies. Stick with water. Avoid all carbonated drinks, because the last thing you want to do on TV is burp! Stay away from caffeine, too—you may be nervous doing this for the first time, and caffeine will make an already nervous person appear jittery. The same rules hold true for radio appearances.

Don't forget, also, to get your news stories into the hands of prospects, customers, and high-value networking contacts. The same is true for radio and TV—get radio interviews recorded on CD, and TV appearances on DVD. This can be done for a very small fee, if your computer isn't already equipped for it. Just make sure you have permission first, and/or pay the necessary fee, so you don't get into trouble for copyright violations.

THERE'S NOTHING LIKE BEING AN AUTHOR

There's one last tactic I'd like to bring up here: writing a book. This isn't as difficult as it sounds, certainly not the daunting task you think it is. In fact, one of my e-books that I've distributed online is merely a collection of many of my articles, and I have hundreds of articles since I write them on a fairly regular basis, as you should, too. It only took a few minutes to compile them all into one e-book.

A book takes you to another level of credibility and expert status that isn't generally available to nonauthors. It's sort of an automatic way of earning guru status. For example, authors can usually get lucrative paid speaking engagements just by virtue of being authors, while nonauthors who wish to pursue a career in paid speaking usually have to do dozens, if not hundreds, of free appearances before pursuing speaking fees. In the end, it's quicker to just write a book!

Like getting news coverage, having your own book isn't as

daunting a task as it sounds. Sure, it will take time and work to write, but it's easy to write on a topic that relates to what you do for a living and that you're very familiar with. In addition, a book needn't be long. My first book was 120 pages and it was a resounding success—and that was a book I sold for a living! You're not doing this to make a living—you're doing it to further establish yourself as an expert and, in turn, to get the media to take you seriously.

The simplest way to start is with an e-book. This is as simple as writing your book in your computer's word processing software, saving it as a .pdf file, and making it available on your web site.

Don't discount the value of e-books. They're considered equal to traditionally published books in today's world and are becoming increasingly as common. In fact, my first book was an e-book and I began to get calls from publishers only seven months after I released it. The best part about an e-book is that it costs virtually nothing to produce. It's also the easiest to distribute—when you want to send it to a prospect, you simply e-mail it to them, and they'll then see how much value you can bring them as an expert author.

The next step up is print-on-demand. This prints an actual book, but instead of having to order quantities of hundreds or possibly even thousands of copies from a printer, you can order as few as one at a time if you so desire. Print-on-demand presses have printing equipment that can produce one book at a time, just like a regular computer printer lets you print only one copy of a document if you want.

Next up from print-on-demand is going to a traditional printer. In this case, you'll need to order in quantity, and that, of course, isn't suitable when you're creating a book for the purpose of building credibility rather than to sell it.

So far, I'm talking about self-publishing: writing and producing the book yourself, without the backing of a publisher. That's because, again, this is for the purpose of building your credibility, not making a living from book sales. However, don't even begin to think that getting picked up by a publisher is out of your reach. After all, before you picked up this book, you probably thought it was impossible to have a story run in Yahoo! News and expert articles written by you published online, but now you know how to make that happen overnight. You probably thought it was impossible to get reporters writing about you within a week or two, but that also is totally within your reach, if you'll take the steps to attain it. Likewise, getting a book published is not impossible. Doing all of these things to establish yourself as a recognized expert will get you far. Don't forget, doors will open to you as an expert that you didn't even know existed.

Our purpose here, of course, is to use a book to make you more media-friendly and attractive. Having the word *author* after your name creates assumed expertise and makes it all the easier to get media attention and the respect of reporters. When I respond to news queries from reporters, my status as an author instantly puts me ahead of other sales experts who respond. (Why they don't self-publish books of their own is beyond me.)

One last word on books: Did you know that registering to sell your book on Amazon.com is almost as easy as registering to sell on eBay? You can even sell e-books there! Having your book listed on Amazon will go a long, long way toward establishing your reputation as a recognized expert, because nearly all people assume that any book on Amazon must be a published book.

Everything in this chapter is designed to further enforce your expert authority in the eyes of others. Media coverage and having your own book, even if it's just an e-book, will naturally generate a large number of leads, get people calling you, and, most importantly, get them to want to buy from you so you won't have to sell them. Also, as I've said, when you do these things, other opportunities you didn't even know about will come your way.

Don't forget to bring your media clippings and book along next time you're up for a promotion, pay raise, or annual review. You can practically name your price when you're a recognized expert whom anyone would want on their staff.

At NeverColdCall.com/Secrets, you'll find more tips and guidelines on how to approach the media, and on creating your own book and using it to ultimately generate sales.

11

Top Sales Pros Are Internet-Savvy

One of the biggest mistakes of salespeople in today's world is the failure to embrace the Internet and to recognize and use its massive capabilities as a lead-generation machine, an extremely powerful sales tool, a publicity generator, and so much more.

I like to call the World Wide Web the World Wide Prospecting Web instead. A solid online strategy by itself can provide you with more business than you can handle. Combine that with everything else you're learning in this book and you'll be unstoppable—you'll become one of the elite of the top sales pros.

Using the Internet to get sales begins with having a web site of your own. I don't mean your employer's web site—I mean your own web site. As I explained in Chapter 8, you've got to think of yourself as owning your own business, your very own sales agency, if you want to achieve the success of a top sales pro.

A company web site is necessary and useful when it comes to showing prospects that they are going to do business with a reputable, financially stable, capable organization. However, it does nothing for you as a salesperson. Very few companies provide their sales reps with individual web sites or pages, so it's important for you to do this on your own initiative.

A web site accomplishes many tasks for you as a salesperson:

- It enable prospects to find you while doing research on-line.
- It displays your credentials up front, letting visitors know you're a recognized expert.
- It gets visitors to sign up for your e-mail newsletter.
- It advertises the benefits of your products or services in a business owner's language—including case studies, if applicable, showing how you've increased someone's profitability.
- It proves your integrity by including testimonials and endorsements from existing customers; proof is a very important part of online marketing.

Before elaborating on those points, let me tell you up front that creating a web site, like many of the other things you're learning in this book, is easy and is certainly not out of reach for you. Many tools are now available online that will allow you to have a site up and running in minutes, for as low as a few dollars per month (you can find links to many of these low-cost services at NeverColdCall.com/Secrets). And remember, implementing these strategies will always be far, far easier than going through life selling, trying to cold call, overcoming objections, using closes, having your manager breathing down your neck, and everything else that comes with selling. We're here to get prospects to buy!

In addition to online web site creation services, there are Microsoft FrontPage and Adobe Dreamweaver, both of which are known as "what you see is what you get," or WYSIWYG (pronounced "wizziwig"), editing programs. In other words, you don't need to know any code or programming language to use these. They're just like using a word processor or Power-Point—you type in what you want, copy and paste the graphics and photos, and what you see on your screen is exactly what will show up in the online version of your web site.

In addition, there are thousands of free and low-cost templates for both of these programs available for download online, so creating a site can be as simple as downloading a template, typing in your text, pasting graphics, and uploading your new site to a web hosting company.

Before even creating your site, though, you'll need to reserve a domain name for it. A domain name is what people type into their Web browsers to get to your site; for example, NeverCold Call.com is the domain name for one of my sites. Choose something that's easy to remember, but you don't have to be too picky about it. After all, your Web address will be printed on all of your materials, so it's not like you're asking people to memorize it.

As to the structure of a web site, you have two goals for every visit a prospect makes to your site:

1. To provide information—to establish your credibility, provide testimonials, and so on.
2. To capture the prospect's name and e-mail address.

I'm going to start by discussing point number two, because that's something you'll want to happen as soon as prospects enter your site and before they begin reading.

The importance of capturing prospects' names and e-mail addresses as they visit your site is enormous—it enables you to maintain ongoing contact with prospects rather than having a one-time interaction that goes nowhere. I'll now cover the how-to part of capturing names and e-mail addresses.

Naturally, people are fed up with spam and junk mail and endless messages from all of the lists they already subscribe to; therefore it takes a lot more than simply saying, "Sign up for my free newsletter," to get people to join.

What you need to do to get people to subscribe is to offer them an incentive to sign up, something they can access immediately. The desire for instant gratification is alive and well in today's world and you'll need to use it to your advantage rather than fight it. Instead of saying, "Sign up for my free newsletter," what you want your site to say is, "Get instant access to my free _____." Fill in the blank with whatever your particular giveaway happens to be.

On NeverColdCall.com, I offer visitors to the site the opportunity to download the first 10 chapters of my home study course, *Cold Calling Is A Waste Of Time: Sales Success in the Information Age*, absolutely free. This is a tremendous value because, at the time of this writing, the retail price for that product is $97. People recognize the value of getting the first

10 chapters, complete and unedited, for free, and especially if they are considering purchasing that product. Those free chapters are like a test-drive.

As a result of my offering that free download, several hundred people sign up for my newsletter each day. Compare that to when I didn't offer a free download—I simply said, "Sign up for my free newsletter." When I just did that, I only got about 50 sign-ups per day.

Right now you're probably realizing the importance of having a free e-book of your own, as discussed in Chapter 10. An e-book not only brands you as an author and gives you a level of credibility you could not get otherwise, but it also gives you a fabulous incentive to get prospects to willingly give you their names and e-mail addresses, along with permission to send them your newsletter!

There are a lot of variations on the concept of an e-book that are especially effective for salespeople. Using a couple of different industries as examples, here are some e-book and report titles that I've seen salespeople use successfully to build a large newsletter list:

- "Seven Steps to Financial Freedom for Families"
- "Seven Steps to Building a College Fund for Your Children"
- "Seven Steps to Finding—and Getting—Your Dream Home"
- "Seven Steps to Increased Profitability in Widget Manufacturing"

. . . and so on.

In case you're wondering about all the "Seven Steps" listed here, there is something in marketing known as "The Law of

Sevens and Nines." Credit goes to Mark Joyner for teaching me that. It states that prices and other numbers used in marketing, such as in book titles, that contain the numbers seven and nine pull much better than numbers that do not. For example, products priced at $97 consistently sell better than products priced at $99, *or* $95—even though $95 is obviously less expensive! This is why I like "Seven Steps" as part of the title for e-books and other promotional reports.

When you create your free e-book or free report, remember Frank's Rule Number One when it comes to writing free giveaway products for your prospects: When writing e-books, reports, or other giveaways for prospects, your document *must* consist only of useful, helpful information and *must not* contain a sales pitch!

Salespeople—and all other marketers, for that matter—get themselves into trouble because they mistakenly think a free e-book is merely an opportunity to get a sales pitch in front of prospects. Nothing could be further from the truth.

Here are the real reasons to write a free document for distribution to prospects:

- *To establish your credibility as a recognized expert.* I've already covered this in great detail so I won't go over it again here; however, can you imagine receiving an e-book from a respected expert that was nothing but a sales pitch? Of course not. An e-book from a recognized expert contains only valuable information of interest to prospects, as should yours.

- *To keep your name in front of prospects.* If your e-book or report is truly valuable and informational for prospects, they will keep it—which means, of course, that they are also keeping your name and contact information nearby. Believe me, this is far more effective than passing out pens or calendars with your name and number printed on them! A big part of my sales strategy, especially my lead-generation strategies, is to do things that keep the salesperson's name in front of prospects for the long term. This is much more desirable and more effective than doing something like mailing a letter or making a cold call, both of which give prospects an easy way to say no, and neither of which creates any long-term effect beyond the one minute the prospect experiences each.

- *Viral marketing.* Don't let the term scare you—viral marketing simply means word-of-mouth marketing that is strengthened by giving the prospect one or more tools to actually make it happen.

Word-of-mouth marketing is perhaps the best kind, because people tend to believe and trust what their friends tell them. (Word-of-mouth and referrals are pretty much one and the same, by the way.) The problem is getting people to give you good word-of-mouth marketing—all you can do is hope they'll do it. There's no way to force them or demand it.

Enter viral e-books. One of the great things about a free e-book, if it's good, is that people will send it to their friends and colleagues. They're giving you word-of-mouth advertising because your e-book gives them a simple mechanism to do so. People are far more likely to forward a copy of an e-book than they are to pick up the phone and tell their friends about you—similar to how people forward e-mail jokes to their friends all the time, but will almost never call their friends and actually tell the joke. (By the way, jokes are actually used as a viral tool by undesirable people in our society, namely, those who spread viruses and spyware over the Internet. They know people forward jokes so they hide spyware and viruses in the joke e-mails. This is a horrible use of viral marketing, but it's a great example of its effectiveness nonetheless.)

To get people to send your free report to their colleagues, it's helpful to include a statement right on page one telling them that it's okay to do so. Mine says, "This e-book may be sent to your friends, given away as a bonus with products, or distributed in any other manner, as long as it is delivered unchanged via this file and as long as it is not sold at any price." (Thanks, once again, goes to Mark Joyner for teaching me that bit of genius.) This is helpful because many people will worry about violating your copyright if they forward the work to others; this short statement will let them know it's okay.

Now, let's take things a step further: Remember when I said that several hundred people sign up for my newsletter each and every day? It's not just because I give away a big chunk of a $97 product for doing so; it's also because of what people see *after* they enter their name and e-mail address at NeverColdCall.com. After clicking "Submit," they are taken to a page that says, "Wait—before I send you your free e-book, give me the e-mail addresses of three friends, and I'll also send you these three valuable products for free, as my way of thanking you."

The three free gifts are sales training audio programs, downloadable in MP3 format, that people can listen to on their computers or iPods, or burn to CD. I could easily sell these programs for $47 to $97 each on CD through my web site, so people see the value and they tell their friends about me. In fact, about 50 percent of all the people who join my newsletter list also enter the real e-mail addresses of three friends! Those people then visit my site, and the process starts all over again. That's a big reason my site has grown as fast as it has, and why I've become so successful as an author so quickly—it's all thanks to the viral marketing mechanism that's at work on my site.

Setting up a "tell your colleagues" page like this is simple. I show you where to get free resources to do that quickly and easily, via the link at the end of this chapter.

Considering all of this, here are the reasons why your e-book must contain only valuable information and must be devoid of any sales pitches:

- Establishing your credibility as a recognized expert: Obviously, no one will think you're a recognized expert if you're merely sending them a sales pitch.
- Keeping your name in front of prospects: No one will save your e-book on their computer, or print it, if they find no value in it. People avoid sales pitches; they don't embrace them.
- Viral marketing: People will definitely not forward a sales pitch to their friends. They'll only forward good, solid information that they believe will legitimately help their friends.

One last thing: Your e-book must also contain a link to your web site. The entire point of getting people to forward your e-book or free report to others is to get those others visiting your site and entering their contact information as well, so don't overlook this important detail.

As to the mechanics of putting a form on your site where people can enter their information in return for your free e-book and newsletter, mailing services provide cut-and-paste forms you can easily add to your site. I use Pro-Mailer.com; in addition, the link at the end of this chapter will take you to a place where you can find all of the resources you'll need to make this happen.

That covers the subject of getting prospects to give you their name and e-mail address so you can get them on your newsletter list and stay in touch with them for the long term. The other goal of getting people to your site is to provide them with information about you, your credibility, and how you can help them.

The first rule of a web site is to keep it simple. Think back to the "KISS Test" if you've read my previous books; KISS is an acronym for "Keep it simple, stupid!" Nothing will scare site visitors off and make them click the "back" button on their browser faster than a web site that is overcomplicated or that has an annoying flash intro page, rather than taking them directly to a home page they can actually use.

The main goal of your home page, of course, is to get people to sign up for your newsletter and to download your free e-book, along with other giveaways if you use the "tell your friends and get these free gifts" concept. With that in mind, I recommend a very simple layout, where getting people to sign up is the main focus of the page. Take a look at NeverColdCall.com for a great example—I tested endless site layouts and variations to find the most effective one, which is now my home page.

Notice that I use the titles "*New York Times* Bestselling Author" and "Amazon #1 Bestselling Author" liberally throughout the page, and I also include a client testimonial as well as an endorsement from another best-selling author on the page. This is to establish my credibility as a recognized expert, which must be one of your goals as well if you want your home page to be effective.

Let's take a closer look at the client testimonial on my home page. Notice that it isn't overly general, such as "Your newsletter is great!" It's specific, and touches on the specific benefits that particular client has received as a result of reading my newsletter: "Your sales advice is hands-on and practical . . . your selling tips are practical and can be used immediately." That sort of testimonial is much more powerful than a generic one, such as "I think your newsletter is great and I recommend it to others."

In addition, you'll also see that the testimonial includes a photograph of that client. A picture establishes a degree of credibility that the testimonial is real, from a real person, and isn't made up. There is a big problem online of people using fake testimonials, so anything you can do to prove that yours are real will help to overcome any doubts. Audio and video testimonials are very effective as well, for the same reason.

Pick out your favorite customers, the ones you did a really great job for and who appreciate you and love what you've done for them. Those are the customers to obtain testimonials from. When you ask them for testimonials, offer to write the testimonials for them and simply get their approval on them. Many people are busy, not inclined to write, or both, and will appreciate the gesture, especially your star customers who love you and would do anything for you.

Next, let's move on to the author endorsement at the bottom of my home page. Again, this isn't generic, like "What a great read—I highly recommend this book to others." It says,

"If you want to cure your business of the disease of cold calling. . . ." That's specific. It's telling people that my book can put an end to cold calling for them. It addresses a specific benefit of the book, and that's what will get people to gladly type in their name and e-mail address.

One more thing—you'll notice, when you visit my home page, that a short video from me automatically begins to play when you enter the page. It's there because it has dramatically increased the sign-up rate on that page. It's short and to the point—it simply asks visitors to enter their name and e-mail address to get the 10 free chapters—but it is powerful. It's powerful because, as you now know, one of the hallmarks of top sales pros is that they are real. They come across as real people who can relate to other real people, not as automatons who spit out canned lines, which, unfortunately, is exactly how most salespeople come across when meeting with a prospect.

The video on my home page helps to convey to site visitors that I am a real person. They feel a personal connection, rather than just looking at a computer screen. The inclusion of my voice and my photo on the page create that connection. And yes, in case you're wondering, a photograph of you on your home page is a must. Have one taken professionally if need be, but get a good one up there.

The structure of your site, like mine, should be kept simple. Again, simple sites get results, while overcomplicated sites do not. They merely scare people away. A menu bar across the top or in the left column, depending on your site layout, should contain links to only a few pages: an "About Me" page, a page describing the benefits of your product or service, and of course a "Contact" page are must-haves.

I don't advise having much, if any, information about your company on your "About Me" page, unless of course you're a business owner and you're using this information to create a site for your business. For everyone else, that page is to tell people about *you* and *your* credibility; remember, you're running your own business here, and this web site is yours.

In addition to one or two brief paragraphs describing your background and possibly your education, you'll want to include the following on your "About Me" page:

- Links to your press releases/news stories.
- Links to your published articles online (i.e., EzineArticles .com and others).
- Testimonials from customers that describe what *you've* done for them, rather than what your *product* has done for them; for example, "With Frank's help, we were able to increase our productivity and profitability" or "Frank made getting our dream home a reality."
- Link to and/or cover shot of any book, e-book, or reports you've written, including a link to your book on Amazon if you've registered with them to sell it.

When you write the paragraphs that will tell others about you, the most important thing is to include references to your credibility. You might write, "John Doe, author of several articles published on dozens of web sites, has been cited in multiple news stories as an authority on the Widget industry." (If that sounds far-fetched, remember, all you need to do is write a few articles and upload them to article directories, issue a couple of good press releases, and your statement will be true.)

In addition, include references to what you've done for your clients, such as "John has shown many companies how to increase their profitability." If you want business owners calling you, your bio must be written in the language of a business owner, meaning you must talk about having gotten results for others in one or more of the three main business goals. Business owners only respond to results.

Your product page, again, must talk about results and benefits, not features and vague promises. Here is where you want to include testimonials for the product itself, rather than for you as a salesperson. As always, testimonials from your best customers, especially if you can include a photo, will be the most effective. Video testimonials are also a great option if you own or have access to a camcorder. Posting them on your web site is very simple and can be done with free software that's included on most computers today (Windows Movie Maker is bundled with most editions of Microsoft Windows and iMovie is included with all new Macs, as of this writing).

As you can see, no salesperson should be without a web site. Even if your company has a site, and I'm sure it does, you need your very own, to generate leads for you, establish and build on your credibility, and get people to tell others about you.

At NeverColdCall.com/Secrets, you'll find a long list of resources on everything that's been discussed in this chapter, including web site design, creation, and hosting; getting a domain name; adding photos, audio, and video to your site; using newsletter sign-up forms and tell-a-friend forms on your site; and so much more. You'll also find tips and advice on how to promote your site so prospects can easily find it.

12

TOP SALES PROS GIVE FIRST AND GET LATER

There is a lot of talk in the sales world about the concept of value, and I mention it myself quite a bit. So what exactly is value?

Before I answer that, let me tell you what value is *not*. As far as I'm concerned, a typical *value proposition* does not relate to my definition of value whatsoever. Value propositions, as used in the sales world, are slick statements designed to be used in cold calls and in marketing campaigns, supposedly to show the prospect on the other end of the phone that you are capable of delivering tremendous value to them.

The problem with a value proposition, as I see it, is that it is nothing but an offer, a quid pro quo. It's really just a description of the benefits you propose to deliver to the prospect, written in a slick, sales-oriented way that's on the same level as elevator speeches. In other words, you're stating what your offer is—what you can deliver in return for payment—and positioning it in such a way that it sounds more enticing to a prospect than a straight offer does.

My problem with value propositions is that they presuppose payment from the customer in advance of delivering any value. While it's of the utmost importance to have an exceptional offer, something that's far better than what your competition proposes, an offer is not the same thing as value.

Value, to me, is what you deliver to prospects *without any expectation of payment or compensation whatsoever*. It's what you provide above and beyond what you're paid to do. Value, to me, cannot exist with conditions; it cannot be contingent upon payment.

The reason you must position yourself as a recognized expert in order to become a top sales pro is because prospects know that recognized experts deliver value above and beyond the offer; in other words, the offer is separate and distinct from the value you can provide. The offer is the product or service they're paying for. Value is what you deliver above and beyond that. It's what you can do for your customers that they're *not* paying for and that you are not required to do. Recognized experts are seen by customers as trusted business advisers; as such, they bring extra value to the interaction, much more so than an average, nonexpert salesperson can.

When you create a web site and provide links to useful articles and offer a free, helpful report to prospects, you are delivering *value* above and beyond what they would ever get from anyone else. How many salespeople do you know who take the time to write articles and e-books that can help prospects, even prospects who may very well never buy? I hardly know any salespeople who do that—I'm willing to guess that you don't know any either. Delivering that level of information to prospects, with no requirement or expectation of payment, is *value*.

When you put your customers in touch with each other, in a way that they can communicate and collaborate about how to best take advantage of the solutions you provide, you are providing *value*. Manufacturers set up user groups for their products; why don't salespeople? The reason I provide access to private online discussion forums for buyers of my products is simply because the ideas and knowledge they can gain from other users of my products can easily exceed the value they get from the actual product itself.

When you're honest with a prospect and state that your solution may not be the most appropriate for them, and that a competitor's may be better, you're delivering a level of *value* that's practically nonexistent in the sales world. This kind of value—the purest form of integrity—is so rare that prospects will frequently buy your less-than-ideal solution rather than the competitor's solution that you'd recommended, just to get you on their side and to have access to you as a trusted business adviser.

Value is rare, and, as a result, it's in extremely high demand. If you can deliver value to your prospects, you, too, will be in extremely high demand. Word will spread fast, and your phone will ring off the hook with hot referrals. Delivering value is something that all top sales pros do. It's something that will certainly bring you success if you do it, and will keep you down if you don't do it.

Considering the level of value that most salespeople provide—practically none at all—can you see why the standard advice of "Close the sale and ask for three referrals" almost never works? If you haven't delivered value, customers have no reason at all to refer anyone to you, and, quite honestly, you have no right to ask for referrals if you have not delivered value. Everything comes at a price—there is no such thing as something for nothing, and one must not expect something for nothing. If you haven't delivered value, you don't deserve referrals—plain and simple. However, if you deliver value, referrals will just come to you. You won't even have to ask for them.

I once worked with someone who delivered the most value I've ever seen a salesperson deliver. He was more than willing to take as much time as necessary with prospects to make sure they got not only the right solution from him but any other assistance and advice he could provide to them about their businesses. Also, he did not hesitate to drive out to a customer's location when they needed his assistance, whether it was related to his product or not.

As a result of all this added value, which he delivered at no cost and with no expectation of payment or compensation, he constantly had more referrals coming to him than he could handle. It got to the point where he'd pass the excess leads on to other reps in the office and offer to split the commission with them.

This gentleman's commission check was always above five figures, every month, yet he never spent one single minute prospecting, marketing himself, or doing anything else to find leads. The flood of referrals he received was solely due to the *value* he delivered to his customers.

What can you do, today, to begin delivering value to your prospects and customers? I'm talking about value that you deliver, in person, as a result of things you do for prospects and customers that are not required of you. You're most definitely going to deliver value as a result of your articles, free reports, and e-books; the confidence prospects will have in you due to your expert status; and the useful information you'll provide to others while you're speaking. However, what can you do, starting today, to deliver value to those who haven't even bought yet—and possibly never will—without expectation of payment or reward?

I've mentioned my co-worker who was always there for his customers, to help them with whatever they needed, and never letting them call the customer support hotline where they'd be billed for requesting assistance. I began doing the same thing after I saw how successful he was, just for delivering value by going the extra mile for customers. I got out of the habit of avoiding doing things for prospects, and began offering to do them myself, for free, instead. Up to that point, when prospects had met with me not because they had a current need to buy a major product but because they needed some minor work or assistance that would pay me little or no commission, I had always given them the toll-free number they could call to schedule a technician to come out and help them with whatever the issue happened to be. Service calls resulted in a visit charge, plus hourly fees, with a one-hour minimum, even if it was something small that could be completed in a few minutes, so they wound up being potentially very costly.

Then I took a new approach. Instead of continuing to say, "Call the 800 number," I put some basic tools in my car and familiarized myself with the most basic jobs and service requests that customers might have. I then took the extra 5 or 10 minutes to do it myself when people asked for help with those particular issues.

The result? People appreciated the value I was now providing. They knew full well that service calls were expensive; they knew full well that I was not being paid to help them—after all, I was taking time out of my day that could be spent getting sales and earning commissions and was therefore potentially losing money; and, most importantly, they knew full well that I was not at all required to help them. My job, in those cases, merely required me to give them the toll-free support hotline.

I instantly transformed my image and reputation from that of a salesperson to that of a trusted business adviser. People didn't just call me to buy anymore—they called me for my help, my advice, my opinion. Oh yeah—they did still call to buy from me, a lot more than they had before. In fact, word started to spread like wildfire, and soon I was reaping the rewards of what I'd started doing, in the form of endless referrals!

Remember, most people have very low expectations of salespeople. This is because of the sad fact that most salespeople do not deliver any value whatsoever, have no desire to, and never will. They just want a commission check. Remember the difference between persuasion and manipulation? (If not, see Chapter 2.) People's expectations are set so low that when you come into the picture, delivering tremendous value, they'll practically give anything for the opportunity to work with you instead of all your manipulative competitors.

I'd like to pause for a moment here and quickly recap all the ways you've learned so far to be different from every other salesperson out there:

- You will be a persuader, not a manipulator. Other salespeople will continue to use slick sales lines, pushy selling techniques, and closes designed to manipulate prospects into signing.
- You will not harass people with annoying cold calls. Other salespeople will go on cold calling, wasting people's time and annoying them.
- You will have the image and persona of a powerful business leader, the kind who inspires trust and confidence in prospects. Other salespeople will continue on with the stereotypical image of a salesperson, the kind who uses canned lines and questions instead of real conversation, comes off as needy and nervous, and who would never, ever be thought of as a trusted business adviser.
- You will go to networking events as an informed speaker and leader. Other salespeople will continue to show up, stand around, and socialize, without ever meeting real decision makers.
- You will have an endless supply of hot referrals thanks to your professionalism, integrity, and knowledge of how to secure qualified referrals. Other salespeople will continue to ask for three referrals after every sale, and never get any good ones because they haven't done anything to deserve them.
- You will think and talk like a knowledgeable business owner, and that will make other business owners like you want to work with you. Other salespeople will continue to

ask totally irrelevant questions, make themselves appear foolish by giving business owners advice that is dead wrong, and fail to deliver profit-justified solutions that would actually make an improvement.

- You will become a competent public speaker and use your skills to make a name for yourself. Other salespeople won't learn how to become great speakers. They'll continue to run appointments in weaker voices, and will never get up on platforms and behind podiums to make themselves visible and accessible to the business community.

- You'll become a recognized expert in your field, and will be able to back that status up with published articles and news items that will have prospects vying for the opportunity to work with you. Other salespeople will have no status and will continue to be seen by prospects as greedy pests who are not able to provide any valuable knowledge and advice. They'll continue to make 50 calls a day to try to scrape up business because they're not the ones getting media exposure, and therefore business contacts and sales.

- You'll create a web site and online marketing strategy that runs on autopilot to generate hot leads for you and to spread the word about you and your credibility. Other salespeople will still whine and complain that they don't have any good leads and will go on making those 50 cold calls per day with few results, instead of taking the time to build something that actually gets results.

- You'll provide value to others and, as a result, they will reciprocate with business and referrals. Other salespeople will run out the door every time they know they won't get an immediate sale and will never reap anything.

As I read through this list, I recognize one theme that is part of each and every point: value. Everything on that list delivers value, in one way or another, to your customers and prospects. Everything on that list—each item being a different secret of top sales pros—delivers the level of value necessary to create a top sales pro. So if I had to sum up all the information in this book and explain in a single sentence what top sales pros do differently that makes them so successful, I'd have to say that top sales pros deliver value, while average salespeople do not.

The great thing about implementing the inside secrets of top sales pros is that doing so will not only make you wildly successful but it will also benefit your customers to an amazing degree. It's the perfect win-win situation.

There are a lot of theories out there about why delivering value first, with no payment and no expectation of payment, is so effective. Ralph Waldo Emerson wrote an essay on the law of compensation, which states that nature has checks and balances and no deed, good or bad, goes unrewarded. Napoleon Hill talked about the principle of going the extra mile, and how going the extra mile makes you so indispensable that people will want to work with you above all others. There are theories that delivering value to others without expectation of reward causes you to attract or manifest those rewards and overall success in your life.

I personally don't know which theory, if any, is the correct one, but I do know that giving value first *works*. I don't have to know how it works, as long as I know that it works. After all, most people don't know how cars or computers or televisions work, but they are able to use them anyway.

For more on the principle of achieving success and attaining massive sales by giving value first, see NeverColdCall.com/ Secrets, where you will learn more about ways you can give value first.

13

TOP SALES PROS BUILD COMMUNITIES OF PROSPECTS

Have you ever noticed that manufacturers, particularly of computers, video cameras, and other high-tech devices, will create or help to create user groups? Have you ever wondered why they do that? They do it simply because creating a user group creates a community of owners and prospective owners of those products. Creating such a community achieves two goals:

1. Members of these communities are able to brainstorm, share ideas, and help each other to benefit most from the products, which results in very high customer satisfaction and the discovery of new and innovative uses for the products.

2. Even more importantly, creating communities of both existing and prospective customers makes it easy for word-of-mouth to begin to spread. Groups of users who converse and share ideas among themselves begin to tell others about the group and the product. This begins a buzz about the product and initiates the spread of word-of-mouth. Communities, in this case, become a mechanism that enables viral marketing to take place.

I devoted Chapter 6 of this book to getting referrals, I recommended another book entirely for detailed information on how to get referrals, and I also offer free tips and advice on my web site about how to get referrals. Why is it necessary to go through all of this, just to learn how to get referrals? Quite simply, it's because in order to get a quality referral, your customers must take some sort of action that will be for your benefit. Granted, when you do the job and deliver the value of a top sales pro, customers will give you referrals—even more so than before—but the point is that they're doing it because it will benefit their friends and not themselves.

How can you get people talking about you other than through referrals? What about prospects you haven't had the chance to help yet, who don't have anything buzz-worthy to tell their friends about? A great way to accomplish this is to build a community where your prospects and customers can get together, share ideas, and brainstorm, all with you as their fearless leader.

Building a community can take a lot of forms. You can host get-togethers once a month—I know top real estate agents who host parties for their clients on a regular basis. You can host events that are fun and educational for your customers—many high-end car dealerships sponsor outings where customers can drive and enjoy new vehicles. Many business owners also host online discussion forums, where customers and prospects alike can interact, ask questions, and explore opportunities to use the products.

That latter choice is what I happen to use: an online discussion forum. On that site, people can browse the different categories in the forum, read posts and replies, and, of course, post their own questions and responses to other people's questions.

This brings *value*—there's that word again—in a few different ways to prospects who don't yet own my products. First of all, they get to talk firsthand with people who already own my products. How many times do prospects ask for references who they can call to make sure what you're offering is legitimate? A discussion forum takes care of that issue, because prospects who want references can just communicate directly with customers.

Second, prospects can learn and benefit from my products indirectly, through the knowledge of those who already own and use them. This is a huge dose of added value, because most people who do what I do are secretive about the content of their products and would prefer to withhold all the content to everyone but paying customers. However, we've seen what giving value first without expectations can accomplish, and so I choose to do that in my discussion forums by letting my clients and customers talk to the outside world about what I teach.

Finally, and perhaps most importantly, customers gain a tremendous amount of added value by being able to communicate directly with each other, talk about how they are using the products to the greatest benefit, and share and create additional uses and ideas. To many customers, this is more valuable than the content of the product itself. (It's also why I get frustrated when people don't take advantage of my discussion forums. They're really missing out on a lot.)

As you can see, creating an open community where your prospects as well as your customers can communicate for their mutual benefit is very effective both in providing value to them and as a viral marketing mechanism, so they can spread the word about you and your solutions to others.

What's the best format to do this? Well, there is no *best* way, but there are several options open to you.

ONLINE DISCUSSION FORUMS

I like this one the best to get started right away. It's not necessarily the only option you should be using, and in rare cases it may not be effective at all; however, it's something you can get up and running right away, and toward which you can immediately start directing people to get them participating.

There's another hidden benefit to having an online discussion forum of your own, and that's the power it has in impressing prospects. Think of the impact the following statement will have on a prospect at the conclusion of an appointment: "By the way, I run an online discussion forum where several of my customers participate and discuss my products they're using, share ideas on them, and where I drop in and answer their questions and concerns. Feel free to log in and take a look around, and see what people are talking about. The Web address is _____."

You can also provide your forum address to prospects in advance of an appointment. Instead of sending out the old-school information letter or confirmation, you can direct prospects to your online forum.

Can you see how powerful this is, how impressive it is to prospects, and how it will completely obliterate your competition and leave them with no chance at all of getting the sale? Again, you're giving value before even making an offer for prospects to buy from you. Value that's given first, without compensation, goes a long way toward making you highly successful. Combine that with the immediate and direct effects of a discussion forum—the fact that prospects can see firsthand that people are benefiting from your solutions, and that you provide value to your customers via the forum—and your worth in the prospect's eyes becomes immense. They will want to do business with you, and no one else.

There's another huge tactical advantage that a discussion forum gives you. Instead of coming out and saying it, let's see if you can figure it out: Have you ever posted a message on a discussion forum, and then found yourself coming back over and over again to see what others said in response to your post? I know I do! I always revisit discussion threads that I've either posted or replied to, in order to find out what others had to say about my post.

The advantage here is that people who have posted on forums come back repeatedly to check responses! This is huge. You probably have no idea how much time Web designers and Internet marketers spend agonizing over how to get people coming back to their sites as repeat visitors.

A discussion forum does that for you automatically. And every time they come back they're reminded of you—they see your name as the forum leader, and see more and more credibility in you due to the fact that you are running that forum. Don't underestimate the power of discussion forums as networking venues. I've been to events and seminars where I've met other business owners and authors from around the world, with whom I'd been communicating in forums for months or even years! If you can provide that to others, they'll provide you with all the sales you need, and more.

One last benefit of a discussion forum—true, in fact, for all of these methods—is that putting your prospects and customers in touch with each other creates a brand-new networking opportunity for them. They'll be happy that they can easily connect with others who have similar interests and concerns, and they will greatly appreciate you for it. It scores even more points in terms of the value you're providing to them.

Creating a discussion forum online is easy. Most Web hosting companies have it as a point-and-click option to add to your site, or you can have them set it up for a small fee. The link at the end of this chapter will point you to resources to get you started quickly.

Be sure to provide a link to your discussion forum on your web site, which people will see *after* they've already signed up for your newsletter. This really accelerates the process of converting a site visitor into a customer. Have the discussion forum open in a new window so they don't have to leave your site to visit it. By the way, discussion forums tend to rank well in Internet search results, so that's another big benefit to using them—more and more prospects will be able to find you online and immediately see you as a leader, a recognized expert.

CONFERENCE AND WEB CONFERENCE CALLS

Hosting conference calls monthly, or at some other regular interval, is a great way to get both prospects and customers together, in one place, to discuss ideas, hear announcements and suggestions from you, and to network among themselves. The nice thing about a conference call as opposed to an online discussion forum is that conversations and ideas advance far more rapidly when people are actually conversing in real time, instead of typing a post in a forum and having to wait for replies.

When you host conference calls, position them as your user groups. Encourage your customers to participate so that they can get the most out of their products by discussing them with others who use them. Invite prospects as well so they can see just how happy your customers are, how much value you provide to them above and beyond your expected responsibilities, and, perhaps most importantly, so they can see you in a leadership role, directing an event of this sort. Again, your competition won't stand a chance. Prospects are used to salespeople who do the bare minimum to get by and nothing more.

It's a good idea to get on the call early to welcome and chat with others as they enter the call. Start on time, welcome everyone to the call, and go through any announcements you may have. Once that is completed, move on to the specific topic of that particular call. I like to have something specific to discuss on each call, such as a particular feature of a product, an unusual benefit someone can get from it, or something purely educational. An educational call might, for example, be run by a financial adviser talking about a specific type of investment, or a real estate agent explaining one of the intricacies in the process of home buying. The point is to have a point—don't invite people to a call just to chitchat and have a meaningless conversation. The purpose is to deliver even more value by sharing some knowledge with the participants.

After the educational portion of the call is over, open it up for questions and discussion. Give people the chance not only to ask you questions but to talk among themselves and discuss the ideas. Encourage a lively discussion. Get people thinking, and make sure they get a lot out of the call.

A step up from regular telephone conference calls are Web conferences. I use Web conferences with my private coaching group, as well as on calls that are open to the public from time to time. I love Web conferencing because it gives you the ability to run a call with many added features, and you have total control over the call. The possible features include audio conference, text chat, private text messaging between users, a large presentation window where you can offer a slideshow or PowerPoint presentation to the group as well as any web sites you might want to show them, and more.

You also have lots of control in a Web conference room. Instead of having everyone talking over each other as on a phone conference, you can let people click a "question" button that will flag their name and let you choose one at a time to ask a question. You can even control who can talk and when. Participants can also use the text feature to type their questions and comments to you and to the room. It's really an ideal environment to host conference calls.

Online conference services are full of features and are inexpensive. In the link at the end of this chapter, you'll find services you can begin using immediately to host your own web conferences.

IN-PERSON GET-TOGETHERS

I love this last one because it adds a personal touch that is largely missing from the others. It also creates an ideal networking environment and gives you a chance to practice and perfect your public speaking abilities.

If you can reserve part of your office for an evening, even just a conference room, you can get started with this idea. Many people such as real estate agents host get-togethers in their homes. Sometimes these are businesslike presentations, other times they are cocktail parties. Whatever you feel most comfortable doing to stay in contact with your customers and to let them meet and network with each other is up to you.

As to which of these three ideas you should be using, I'd say all of them. Each has unique advantages and disadvantages, and for that reason you should use all three. You can get a discussion forum started online that's always up and running, 24 hours a day, 7 days a week. You can host a conference or Web conference call once a month. Encourage customers to participate, and invite prospects as well so they can see you in action. You can host in-person get-togethers even less frequently than that, maybe once every several months. Be sure to invite prospects to those as well—your star customers are the ones who will tend to show up more than anyone else, and those are the ones who will talk you up to prospects and tell them how great you are!

In addition, these ideas can be combined with my free seminar lead-generation tactic I've described in previous books, so keep that in mind, too. For resources on how to get started using these techniques, please see NeverColdCall.com/Secrets.

14

TOP SALES PROS AUTOMATE

After my latest book came out, *Never Cold Call Again*, I got a lot of e-mails from people objecting to my recommendation that they hire an appointment setter to find and qualify leads for them.

There are two reasons why I make that recommendation. The first and most basic is that selling and prospecting are two entirely different skill sets. It's stupid to take talented salespeople who are skilled in the actual art of sales itself—the process of doing all the things that a top sales pro does—and expect them to spend their valuable time making cold calls on the phone, trying to scrape up business and generate leads. As one of my managers said, it's ridiculous to have experienced, well-trained salespeople doing the jobs of low-paid telemarketers. On top of that, the best salespeople—the top sales pros—are great at selling, but not great at, and usually not interested in, cold prospecting.

That's the difference between cold calling and hiring the job out to an appointment setter. If a salesperson spends his valuable time on that job, a job which is not the best use of his time and for which he is not the best person, it's cold calling. That's why cold calling is a waste of time for salespeople. It's not a waste of time for an appointment setter, someone who specializes in the task of making phone calls and getting appointments.

In addition, I recommend that you have appointment setters call a list of targeted leads rather than names out of a phone book, or to follow up on mailers that you've done.

The last few paragraphs have already alluded to the second and more important reason to hire out the job of appointment setting to appointment setters, namely time. Time is our most valuable asset, far more valuable than money. As salespeople, we are only paid to make sales. That's what generates our commission checks. We're not paid to do all of the activities, tasks, and chores leading up to a sale. We only get paid for making a sale. If that were not the case, we'd get paid per cold call or per proposal, but I sure don't know of any companies that pay on such a plan.

Because there are only so many hours in a day to make sales—typically eight in the normal workday—doesn't it make sense to spend those eight hours making sales and doing nothing else?

When I say spend those hours making sales, I don't mean all the other activities that lead up to a sale. I mean being face-to-face with prospects, getting sales from them—getting signatures on contracts and picking up checks.

It's possible to do this through automation. Automation is anything you do that puts a task on autopilot—on "set it and forget it"—so that your time is free to just make sales.

Hiring out phone calls to an appointment setter is one example of automation, one that also has an added benefit in the fact that having an assistant make calls for you further enhances your image of power, prestige, and of being a recognized expert, all things that go far toward blowing out your competition in prospects' eyes.

Most salespeople have experienced automation in using lead-management or customer relationship management (CRM) software. It's a lot more efficient than trying to manage index card or business card files and remember whom to call and when. Few companies nowadays do not provide CRM software to their reps.

When I started out building my lead-generation systems, I found that distributing well-crafted fliers did an excellent job of getting people to call me; however, the task of getting them out there into the hands of decision makers was very time-consuming. I quickly hired a flier distribution service that was able to get them out to thousands of businesses in a very short time, and at a price that was well worth the cost, considering what my time was worth and that I could now spend all of it on closing sales instead of prospecting for leads.

Many top sales pros I've worked with have created work flows for their sales processes. What this means is that each step, each individual task in the process of closing a sale, is outsourced. All the top sales pro does is actually close the sale.

For example, I know of a top real estate agent who has entry-level agents run open houses; in fact, this practice is quite common in the real estate industry. He has agents with more experience take prospective buyers out to show properties. Only when buyers express interest in a particular property does he actually take over and work directly with them going forward. This is an amazing process of qualifying leads to the point where he only works with those who are almost certain to buy, or at least make a reasonable offer to buy.

The benefit for the agents beneath him is that they're doing fairly simple tasks—conducting open houses and showing properties—with the knowledge that they will get a chunk of his commission for the sales he closes, and they know very well that he closes almost all of them. After all, he's a top sales pro! He does all of the things I've shown you in this book and is a respected, recognized expert as a result of it all. People look up to him and *want to buy* from him.

Of course, he's splitting his commissions with the other agents who help out with the sales process. However, in spite of this, he's making far more money—several times more—than he could otherwise. Why? Because he spends all of his working hours face-to-face with *buyers*, not lookers! All he does is get sales, all day long!

This process of automation gives him a tremendous amount of leverage, and leverage is something that all top sales pros use to their advantage. *Leverage* simply means the use of another person's time or talents to get a job done for you. When I hired a flier distribution service, I was using leverage—the leverage of their time and their ability to get the job done far better than I ever could on my own.

When I hired appointment setters, I was again using the leverage of their time. The several hours it took to make those phone calls were freed up in my schedule and I spent those hours meeting face-to-face with the people who were qualified on those phone calls. All I did was get contracts and checks.

When that real estate agent has lower-level agents doing most of the work for him, he is using the leverage of their time and their talents as well. They free up his schedule to do nothing but close, and he also gains the advantage of their sales abilities in order to get people to the point of making an offer.

As you go through your day, analyze every single task you do, and ask yourself if it's something that you could have someone else do in order to free up your time. For each task, ask yourself if it's worth taking you out of the field and away from a potential meeting with someone who wants to buy.

In my business, I've hired out just about every task I had previously been doing myself. That's why I have time to sit here and write this book. My time is now entirely devoted to thinking, creating new books and other products, and to my coaching and learning program—in fact, without the leverage of other people's time to handle my everyday tasks, I would never have been able to start a coaching program, and people have been asking for it for a long time.

By setting up a lead-generation web site, you automate part of the task of finding new prospects as well as the task of establishing your credibility with them.

Remember, top sales pros automate. They don't do any work that isn't worth their time, time that could be spent closing sales and nothing else. At NeverColdCall.com/Secrets you'll find more examples of automation as well as resources that will enable you to start automating, immediately.

15

TOP SALES PROS
BUILD AND
USE SYSTEMS

This concept is similar to that of automation, yet different. Building and using systems has to do with taking all of the individual tactics and techniques—the inside secrets of top sales pros, as well as other elements of your overall sales strategy—and putting them together in an order and in such a way that they work together harmoniously to maximize your results.

As an example, let's consider many of the ideas I've given you in this book, such as:

- Publishing articles online.
- Issuing press releases.
- Getting media coverage and publicity.
- Pursuing public speaking at networking events.
- Creating a web site.
- Using the social dynamics of power and control.

- Giving value first.
- Learning to think like a business owner.
- Learning to persuade, not manipulate.

Now, let's put those concepts in a logical order to create what I like to call a *system of systems.*

1. *Theory/knowledge.* Some of the items on that list consist of knowledge that you'll need to learn in order to become a top sales pro, or techniques that you'll be using personally, such as the correct body language in appointments. Items in this category include using the social dynamics of power and control, learning to think like a business owner, and learning to persuade rather than manipulate. Because these are things you must learn on your own time, and in advance of becoming a top sales pro, begin immediately to learn and internalize them. I call this your *inner game*—your internal knowledge and confidence that will build a foundation for all of your tactics and techniques, your *outer game*, to work effectively. Having said that, there's no reason not to begin using my other strategies while you're learning, so they come next, in the proper order, of course.

2. *Giving value first.* This is something you can begin doing immediately to reap its rewards. Think about how you can provide value to prospects and customers, even if it's as simple as spending extra time addressing the questions and concerns of someone who is unlikely to ever buy. Start today.

3. *Publishing articles online.* It makes sense to establish yourself as a recognized expert and to create proof of that status before implementing other strategies, because the effective-

ness of those other strategies is greatly multiplied by having those credentials to begin with. Writing and publishing one or more articles online comes at the head of the list of ways to become a recognized expert, because they're free and they're something that you can do right now without any resources other than your own time and knowledge.

4. *Issuing press releases.* Next, it makes sense to issue one or more press releases, and to save and print them once they're issued, along with the news items in Yahoo! News and Google News that they will generate.

5. *Getting media coverage and free publicity.* This comes next in logical order because your chances of accomplishing this one are much, much better when you have on hand published articles and press releases that you use to create a media kit, which you then send out to reporters to get their attention. Notice that everything happens in logical order, rather than you trying to do everything at once.

6. *Creating a web site.* Having your own personal web site comes at this point in the timeline because you can now include links to your published articles, press releases, and other media coverage you get, right on your site. You can also include those expert credentials in your personal bio on the site.

7. *Pursuing public speaking.* I put public speaking last in this example because it will be much easier to get speaking opportunities at networking events when you have your expert credentials in place, along with a web site address that you can print on fliers, business cards, and any other handouts you will provide to audience members at events where you speak.

Again, this is just an example timeline, but it shows you exactly why you must execute your strategies in a logical order that will allow you to build a foundation. Then ensure that each successive strategy builds on the previous ones so that they support you as you add more strategies and continue on the path to becoming a top sales pro.

The same concept holds true no matter what's included in the collective strategies you'll be using. My previous books specifically covered lead-generation strategies and outlined a similar system of systems in order to implement them most effectively. If you're using those techniques as well, combine them with the secrets of top sales pros to build an overall, effective system that gets the most results for you.

At NeverColdCall.com/Secrets, you'll find sample timelines and work flows that will maximize your sales results quickly.

16

TOP SALES PROS
DON'T
USE CLOSES

If there is one thing in the realm of selling tactics and techniques that just reeks of manipulation, it's the idea of using closes to get a sale.

Remember the definition of selling at the beginning of the book? Top sales pros are so effective at delivering value, as well as the right solutions, to prospects that they never have to sell. People just buy from them.

Using closing techniques is the epitome of selling as I define it, and the necessity to use closing tactics shows that you have failed to do your job as a salesperson and to deliver value to the prospect.

If you do all of the things I've explained in this book, and put them together to work as a system of systems, you'll never need to use another close again. Instead, people will be thrilled to buy from you.

With that in mind, let's take a look at some of the closing tactics that are still being advocated, since the old-school sales mentality is alive and well.

- *The alternative close.* I consider the alternative close to be extremely insidious. Unfortunately, it's also one of the most commonly used closing tactics. I hate it because it reeks of manipulation. Instead of showing a prospect value and giving them the opportunity to buy from you, you instead give them a choice of one decision or the other, with the intent being to get them to choose one instead of saying no to both. Another big reason I despise the alternative close is because the job of a top sales pro, or any salesperson with honesty and integrity for that matter, is to determine which solution will be best for a prospect, and to develop that solution and offer it to the prospect. If you are offering a choice of multiple solutions, you obviously haven't done your job of developing the correct one for that prospect! Top sales pros don't manipulate people into choosing one purchase or the other; they provide solutions that create a mutually beneficial, win-win situation for both the salesperson and the customer. Note that this close is used just as frequently in making cold calls as in closing sales; for example, "I can meet with you either Monday or Wednesday. Which day would you prefer?"
- *The bracket close.* This is an even slimier technique than the alternative close. It's simply another version of it, where you offer three choices, with the target choice in the middle. Manipulation at its worst.

- *The Ben Franklin or balance-sheet close.* In this close, the salesperson takes out a sheet of paper and divides it into two columns, labeled "Pros" and "Cons." He then, with the prospect, proceeds to list each pro and each con of making the purchase that day. The most obvious problem with this approach is that you're pointing out all of the cons of buying your product, for the prospect to plainly see! Don't think that having more pros than cons will make the prospect buy; one con alone, if it is powerful enough, can wipe out dozens of pros. The other big problem with this close is that if you even have to make a list of the pros of buying from you, you have failed miserably in delivering value to the prospect. Remember, delivering value first makes closes totally unnecessary.

- *The embarrassment close.* This close is intended to force the prospect to buy in order to save face. For example, when I sold telephone systems, I represented the most expensive company in the world, and we naturally had to deal with a lot of price objections. Some of the sleazier reps in the office would respond to price objections with a smug, "That's okay, we understand that not everyone can afford us." The obvious intent is to shame the prospect into buying in order to prove they can afford it. The reality is that this tactic shows a total lack of integrity on the part of the salesperson and angers plenty of prospects in the process.

- *The yes ladder close.* This close involves asking the prospect a series of questions to which you know they will answer yes. The theory behind it is that once they're in the habit of saying yes to you, they'll say yes when the time comes to ask for the order. In the real world, this simply doesn't work, *if* you have not delivered value. Just because a prospect answers yes to a bunch of silly questions that have nothing to do with the sale and that are designed to force them to say yes doesn't mean they'll agree to buy. It also insults their intelligence. I remember buying a car several years ago and negotiating the price with the salesman. He asked, "Do you want to buy a new car today?" to which I replied, "No, I had nothing better to do and decided to sit in your office to waste some time." Obviously, his trick didn't work on me. The bottom line is that, with or without this tactic, prospects will not say yes to a solution that doesn't benefit them, no matter how much you've tricked them into saying yes leading up to the close.

- *The price-match close.* This close is used a lot in the retail world. Quite simply, you offer to match any competitor's price if they buy from you today. The problem is that you completely devalue your product when you offer to match any price. You're subcommunicating that you and your product are no better than all of your competition and their products, when in reality a top sales pro is able to get top dollar all the time. Prospects are willing to pay top dollar to a top sales pro because he has demonstrated and delivered so much value before ever asking for the order. It's also well-known in the marketing world that products frequently sell better when the price is *raised* and sell worse when the price is dropped. This is because higher prices imply higher value, while low prices imply cheapness and a lack of value.

- *The doubt close.* In this close, you figure out what the prospect likes best about your product, and then you express doubt about that benefit in order to let them tell you how good your product is. Like the balance-sheet close, this is dangerous because you never want to imply that there are any negatives about your product, and you don't want to create doubt in the mind of a prospect who is already excited about buying from you.

Hopefully, as you read through the descriptions of all of these closes, you realized the lesson here: Closes are only needed by salespeople who don't deliver value.

All of the ideas in this book are designed to help you deliver value to prospects—and add value to your own name. Being a recognized expert creates value. Working with prospects to develop win-win solutions creates value. Being powerful and leading prospects to that win-win solution creates value. Offering your knowledge as a speaker at events delivers value. Profit-justifying solutions will have your prospects begging to buy. Learning to think like a business owner delivers value, because only then can you legitimately help business owners. Having a Web presence, including your own informational web site, a newsletter that delivers useful information to prospects, and discussion forums where prospects and customers alike can interact, creates value, far in excess of what your product alone delivers.

Top sales pros deliver value, and that's why they never need to use closes on prospects. Closes are for shysters and charlatans who are out to make a quick buck at their customers' expense. Salespeople who deliver value through honesty and integrity never need to close sales.

That's because people *want to buy* from them.

17

TOP SALES PROS' CUSTOMERS ARE AN EXCLUSIVE CLUB

I've already shown you the importance of creating communities, including online discussion forums, regular conference calls, and in-person get-togethers where prospects and customers alike can mingle, share ideas, and learn how to better use your products and services for the most benefit. In addition, I feel that it's very important to have a similar group that's for customers only.

You know by now that top sales pros deliver a level of value that's unmatched by amateur salespeople, and that goes far beyond both the cost and the benefits of the product itself. In order to deliver even more value to your customers—and to get them talking about you and sending even more referrals your way—I like to create a customers-only group. Plenty of companies offer customer appreciation events as well as incentives that are only available to existing customers. Why can't you do the same thing as a salesperson?

Top sales pros know that referral selling is a cornerstone of sales success. They know that asking for three referrals after every sale isn't enough, and that following up with customers in a casual manner, such as calling to say, "I'm just making sure everything is going well with your purchase," isn't quite enough to have customers telling their friends and colleagues how great you are and that they, too, should buy from you.

Your customer-only plan doesn't have to include anything big or expensive like a company might put on for its customers. Instead, you can do something small, such as hosting a cocktail hour or luncheon that is open only to your customers. This lets you thank them for their business and continued support in a tangible way, and, more importantly, it gives your customers an opportunity to meet and network with other customers, something they'll greatly appreciate.

Another great idea is to put together educational or informational meetings, where your customers can learn things that will help them either in their personal lives or in their businesses, depending on what it is you happen to sell. You can present information to them yourself, sharing useful knowledge that they'll appreciate. You can also have a friend or colleague present. As you become a top sales pro and become a recognized expert, you're going to find your network escalating rapidly. You will find yourself being contacted by, and networking with, other top sales pros, those who do what I teach—provide informational articles and reports, speak at events, and other things that deliver valuable information to others.

Over time, you'll find that your customers will look up to you more and more as a trusted business adviser and practically forget that you're a salesperson. Even though they have bought from you and will continue to send valuable referrals your way, they will consider you an adviser, because top sales pros are seen as expert consultants, not as salespeople.

Implementing all of these secrets of top sales pros will, by itself, transform you into a high-value consultant in the eyes of your prospects and customers. Creating an exclusive club for your customers where they can meet each other and interact with you privately will further reinforce this image, and you will reap the benefits. And, as with most of my strategies, doing this will bring you high-level contacts and amazing opportunities you never dreamed possible.

At NeverColdCall.com/Secrets, you'll find more ideas for creating an exclusive community for your customers that will help you deliver even more value to them, and let you reap the rewards of continued business, endless referrals, and the stellar reputation of a trusted adviser.

18

Now It's Your
Turn to Become
a Top Sales Pro!

If you've made it this far, you've absorbed a lot of new information. I'm sure I've opened your eyes to ideas, strategies, techniques, and possibilities you never even knew were available to you as a salesperson.

Now that you have the knowledge, you have a choice to make: You can put this book away, continue to go on as you were before, and see no improvement in your sales results. If you choose that route, you won't become a top sales pro. But I'm willing to guess that you are not entirely satisfied with your sales results as they are today, because if you were, you probably wouldn't have read this book in the first place.

Your other choice is to put this book down and immediately begin to implement the new ideas you've learned. You can map out your system of systems, plan what you'll do and in what order, and begin—right now. The single most important step to get yourself on the road to becoming a top sales pro is to *implement*. I've shown you what to do; now it's up to you to do it.

Most top sales pros tend to have an aura of mystery about them, because they don't socialize much with the other salespeople in the office. They come to work, keep to themselves, and do what needs to be done. You won't find them going out to lunch with the whole crew, or standing around the break room drinking coffee instead of working. That's because top sales pros are focused—focused on success. They avoid wasting time on things that won't bring them success, and instead focus on things that will bring them success. They manage their time in such a way that they *only* spend time on activities that bring them results.

Top sales pros implement. That's why they're top sales pros. They don't waste time, and they don't procrastinate. If they have the choice of doing something right now or putting it off until tomorrow, they do it—right now.

You now have a choice. You can put this book away and tell yourself that you'll begin to implement these strategies tomorrow, or the day after tomorrow, or next week, or next month. Chances are, if you do that, you'll never implement them, and you'll never become a top sales pro. Or you can begin your journey to becoming a top sales pro right now. I've shown you things you can do today that will get you results tomorrow— literally overnight. Do them—today.

Money follows action. Without action, you won't make any more money than you are today.

What are your goals? What do you want out of life? How much money do you want to make? Where would you like to be able to live? What kind of car would you like to own? Go ahead and name your goals. Now, keeping those goals in mind, think of what kind of salesperson you'll have to be to achieve them.

I'm sure you're picturing one of the very best of the top sales pros, and you're right. That's what you'll need to become, and you now have the knowledge to make it happen.

Remember, when you use the ideas I've given you, you'll not only become a top sales pro, you'll find that opportunities begin to present themselves and doors begin to open up to you that you never knew existed. Look at my life—you would not be reading this book and I would not be a best-selling author today had I not become a top sales pro first.

I've given you the information. It's up to you to begin using it, starting right now. Best of luck, and congratulations to you on taking the important first step to becoming a top sales pro. Here's to your success!

About the Author

Frank J. Rumbauskas Jr. rose from total failure as a sales rookie to spectacular success as a top sales pro, thanks to several years spent in trial and error, learning directly from top sales pros, and constantly developing and trying new ideas.

Author of the best seller *Never Cold Call Again: Achieve Sales Greatness Without Cold Calling* (Hoboken, NJ: John Wiley & Sons, 2006), Frank is a highly sought-after speaker, consultant, and sales coach. Through his books, CDs, and coaching program, he has taught tens of thousands of salespeople, small business owners, and independent professionals how to generate hot leads without cold calling. Frank's blog can be found online at NeverColdCall.com/Blog.

INDEX

Thank you for reading
Selling Sucks!

For a free tool kit that will help you to quickly and effectively implement the ideas you've learned in this book, please visit:

NeverColdCall.com/Secrets

To learn more about Frank's other books and products, his seminars and workshops, and subscribe to Frank's free newsletter full of powerful sales advice, please visit:

NeverColdCall.com